"Ann Ahrens has exquisitely ar̶   ̶   ̶   leads
ies of the faith: that opening c̶   MW00415567
hope, spiritual intimacy, and paradoxically, even joy. If you want
to remember what it was like to be awed by the beauty and majesty
of a loving God who knows you in your darkest hours, read this
book and weep."

—**BRENT ROAM**
lead pastor, One Family Church

"Ann Ahrens writes with the heart of an artist who helps us to
see things in Scripture and in corporate worship that have been
missed by most evangelical churches. Take the time to look and
listen to what she says about the psalms of lament, soul care,
and the community of worshipers as she articulates a beautifully
crafted apologetic for the weekly gathering that goes far beyond
a pep rally for Jesus."

—**JOSEPH R. CRIDER**
Southwestern Baptist Theological Seminary

"This book provides a much-needed resource for today's faith
communities. The contemporary news and social media saturated
world shares pain and suffering without guiding a way forward
other than nihilistic despair or perpetuation of violence. Ahrens'
research breathes life into the chaos through her biblical and
theological examination of lament in a way that local leaders can
honestly apply."

—**JAMES A. LITTLES JR.**
Urshan Graduate School of Theology, emeritus

"As I've followed Ann Ahrens' writing over the last several years, I've found that lament passages are now jumping off the page for me. I'm very pleased that she's ministering similarly to others through this book. The seventeenth-century *Bay Psalm* congregants sang, 'Thy countenance away from us o wherefore dost thou hide?' I trust her scholarship will prompt fresh, biblical, hymnic expression in this vein for our own voices."

—**MARK COPPENGER**
co-editor of *Apologetical Aesthetics*

"One constant in the lives of God's people is that we will experience sadness and suffering. The only question is whether or not we are equipped to cope with it. In this insightful book we discover powerful ways of reclaiming the language of sadness in a way that is thoughtful, biblical, and ultimately healing. This is an important contribution to an area of theology that is fundamental for the life of the church."

—**JOHN SWINTON**
University of Aberdeen

"With sensitivity and clarity, Ann Ahrens writes a groundbreaking biblical foundation and praxis for the church's use of lament in corporate worship. Rooting her study in the Psalms and the life of Jesus, she draws on multiple disciplines and the voices of scholars, pastors, and artists to show why the gathered church needs to lament and how lament rooted in Scriptures fuels genuine praise. Every church staff team needs to read and absorb this book together."

—**ESTHER R. CROOKSHANK**
Southern Baptist Theological Seminary

Suffering, Soul Care, and Community

Suffering, Soul Care, and Community

The Place of Lament in Corporate Worship

ANN AHRENS

Foreword by Eric L. Johnson

WIPF & STOCK · Eugene, Oregon

SUFFERING, SOUL CARE, AND COMMUNITY
The Place of Lament in Corporate Worship

Wipf & Stock
An Imprint of Wipf and Stock Publishers
199 W. 8th Ave., Suite 3
Eugene, OR 97401

www.wipfandstock.com

PAPERBACK ISBN: 978-1-6667-3576-5
HARDCOVER ISBN: 978-1-6667-9318-5
EBOOK ISBN: 978-1-6667-9319-2

01/05/23

For Steve Austin
Beloved friend, gone too soon.

Midway along the journey of our life
I woke to find myself in a dark wood,
For I had wandered off from the straight path.

How hard it is to tell what it was like,
This wood of wilderness, savage and stubborn
(the thought of it brings back all my old fears),

a bitter place! Death could scarce be bitterer.
But if I would show the good that came of it
I must talk about things other than the good.

—DANTE, *THE DIVINE COMEDY*

Contents

Tables and Charts

Foreword

Eric L. Johnson

We all know that negative emotions like anxiety, sadness, shame, and even anger are minimally unpleasant, and they can be terrible. As a result, like all other organisms with negative emotions, humans instinctively seek to avoid them, or at least reduce them (e.g., fear motivates animals to get away from a danger, thus lessening the fear). In addition, many of us were taught from an early age that our negative emotions were not wanted. Shortly after toddlerhood, people around most of us began responding to our crying, anger, or fear by telling us there was no reason to feel that way and to calm ourselves down. There were usually good motives behind these responses. Learning to regulate our emotions is a major accomplishment of childhood and adolescence, and those who don't learn how often end up in very difficult life circumstances. Related to all this, there are strong pressures in most cultures not to display negative emotion in public, and the fact is, much of the Christian community today adds some spiritual pressure: complete trust in God will make your negative emotions disappear. My wife will never forget the declaration she read on a church billboard long ago: "Too blessed to be depressed!"

Yet, as the author of this wonderful book shows, Christianity's canon (*rule*), the Bible, is far more open to the experience and expression of negative emotions than such churches would lead us to believe. Thank God for the Psalms, where we can read the struggles of emotion-exemplars who poured out their hearts before the Lord (Lam 2:19) and modeled for us how to process our negative emotions with God! After all, God made us with our embodied emotion-systems, for he knew we would need negative emotions in a fallen world. Sadness is a fitting response to loss, anger to injustice, guilt to one's wrongdoing. Moreover, a great deal of psychological research has documented the value of being honest about our emotions and expressing them in healthy ways. The Bible even portrays *God* as having negative emotions—though, admittedly, they aren't identical to ours, because he is a spirit and has no body and his emotions are untainted by sin. Perhaps most importantly, as Dr. Ahrens points out, Jesus—the true human— experienced and expressed negative emotions repeatedly throughout his years of ministry, culminating in his last day on earth, framed by his agony in the garden of Gethsemane and his cry of abandonment on the cross, where he identified himself forever with human despair. The Bible itself drives us to the conclusion that we are imaging God when we experience negative emotions. Of course, there are emotions—envy and pride, for example—that are *sinful*. So wisdom is needed to guide us in our emotional experience and expression, just as surely as wisdom is being formed in us through the cultivation of our emotions.

The contemporary church, therefore, desperately needs to read the careful, biblical justification of lament found in this book. Lament is a uniquely Judeo-Christian contribution to contemporary therapy. The goal of life is not to deny our emotions, as the Stoics taught us, or destroy our desire for the Good, as Buddha taught us and contemporary mindfulness subtly underscores. The Bible fosters a God-centered experiencing and expressing of negative emotion that aims at, eventually, surrendering them to God and entering into God's peace and contentment with honesty and integrity. In such ways, we don't deny our humanity, but we fulfill it by living more wholeheartedly, with "transparency before God."

I hope that many pastors and worship leaders will take the lessons and guidelines of this book into their minds and hearts and into their churches. Especially now. For if lament was a fitting response of Jeremiah to the end of the state of Judah, it's certainly appropriate in the midst of the end of Christendom. Even so, lament is never the final word among God's people. Some kind of rejoicing will follow our mourning (Ps 30:5), just as sure as the resurrection of Christ followed his death.

Preface

STUDENTS OF THEOLOGY HAVE long studied the biblical laments, particularly those in the Old Testament, and especially the Psalms. As someone who studied music at the graduate and undergraduate levels, I did not encounter the biblical laments until I decided to attend seminary after realizing that I knew so little about the book by which I lived my life. After taking a course on the theology and practice of worship, I became deeply curious about how much scripture had to say about how and why we worship.

Shortly after beginning my seminary studies, I began to suffer with widespread pain that became so debilitating I had to take a leave of absence from my job. Anxiety, fear, depression, and panic filled my mind as I cried out to God day after day for healing. Church attendance was exhausting as I tried to stand with others around me who were clapping and rejoicing while my body and soul were in agony. While I eventually found a medical solution, my questions around God's silence in my suffering remained. This book was born out of these questions, and the kinship I developed in the process with the writers of the ancient collection of Israel's praises, the Psalms. The Psalms saved me and deepened and broadened my view of God.

Given that so many of the psalms were sung communally, I began to wonder why the themes of lament, protest, and even anger were not part of the corporate worship of the church today. How could this change the way we worship corporately? How many people find corporate worship exhausting, or feel they do not belong because their suffering does not fit with themes of rejoicing, victory, and positive thinking so prevalent in today's singing, preaching, and praying? What change could be affected if we were honest about our suffering and committed ourselves to walk with each other on the long road, whether or not that road ever had a positive ending? How could a practice of corporate lament shape and reshape us more and more into the image of Christ? The more I contemplated these questions, the more I realized that lament was as integral to corporate worship as rejoicing and celebration if we are to be well-formed in the image of Christ. This book is my exploration of these questions, and I offer a foundation upon which worship leaders and pastors can build a practice of lament for their congregation.

I am deeply indebted to the work of biblical scholars such as Walter Brueggemann, Klaus Westermann, John Goldingay, Patrick Miller, and Scott Ellington who have mined the ancient texts of the Psalms and revealed them for the treasures they are. I especially appreciate Timothy Keller's sermon series, *Psalms: The Songs of Jesus*, over which I have wept many times as I listened. Rev. Keller's work on the Psalms has transformed my life. I am also grateful to Eric Johnson, John Swinton, and Curt Thompson who work at the vital intersection of mental health care and spirituality. Their work is baptized in the spirit of the psalmists, and I am humbled at the way they so thoughtfully and holistically care for souls in the way of Christ.

Acknowledgments

SPECIAL THANKS TO RANDALL and Arica DeMerchant, Rebecca Abitt, Scott Ladd, Charles Hubbs, and Jared Runck for the many hours you gave to me on this subject through conversations and emails, for reading drafts and telling me what I needed to hear. I am grateful for Brent and Rebecca Roam for the many ways you show the world who God is in the way you care for and love people unconditionally no matter how difficult the road. To my friend and mentor, Dr. James Littles, I express my deepest gratitude, not only for your exceptional intellect, and for modeling for others how to walk the suffering road, but for challenging me to grow and be more like Christ. Much gratitude and respect goes to Esther Crookshank, my dissertation chair, Joseph Crider, and Eric Johnson, all exceptional scholars who originally guided this study as a dissertation and encouraged me to put it into book form. And to my Lord Jesus Christ, the "man of sorrows and acquainted with infirmity" (Isa 53:3 NRSV). You did not prove your love through power or prestige, but through your wounds. Thank you for the cross. Thank you that it is always safe there.

1

Introduction

"WORSHIP IS NOT PAIN denial, Ann."[1]

The force of my colleague Jared Runck's words felt like a tactical strike. We were standing in the hallway at the bible college where we both taught. Coming from a guest lecture Jared had given in a class I taught on the arts in worship, we were discussing some of the highlights. The force and truth of his words collided head-on with my own inner dissonance around my struggle to understand suffering. I stood there speechless as all my usual responses felt inadequate and hollow. But as I held his statement in my heart during the following weeks, the hollowness I felt gave way to a deep inner longing and an anticipation of a new understanding. I had left that conversation feeling suddenly aware of a treasure I had held in my hands for a long time but was unable to see or understand.

There was another answer, another lens through which to view suffering that was different from my usual lens. The lack of deliverance from suffering, I thought, had always been due to my inability to believe or have enough faith. I began to engage with

1. J. Runck, personal conversation, April 12, 2014.

the Psalms, particularly those that seemed to express such difficult emotions, really hearing their words as if for the first time. The Psalms not only normalized these emotions but called for a deep and painful reexamination of long-held beliefs and patterns of behavior that, instead of keeping me in right standing with God, had made it nearly impossible to know or be known by God. As I began to understand the broad and complex range of emotions found in the Psalms, I experienced simultaneously grief and relief, breaking and healing, as my experiences and beliefs collided head-on. I also began to glimpse a very different view of who God is, one that I could have never seen before. There was no going back, for I had found a "structure to hang pain on," as Rebekah Eklund describes.[2]

When people realize lament is a valid form of communication with God, they are often surprised, amazed, and most unexpectedly, relieved. This should not have to be the case. The practice of lament does not weaken or tear apart a fragile faith; it strengthens, recycles, rebuilds it. This was the aim of the psalmists who uttered such raw and authentic prayers: to lean *into* God by firmly standing on a generations-long relationship with Yahweh that grounded their hope and trust in one who described himself as merciful, gracious, slow to anger, and abounding in steadfast love and faithfulness (Exod 34: 6). These were character traits the psalmists knew to be true about God and traits to which they appealed, either in part or in whole, in nearly every prayer. These prayers, therefore, were not expressions of anti-faith or weakened faith. They were the most trust-filled words the psalmists could utter to one around whom their lives were built. As Eklund states, "Lament inclines toward hope. It leans toward the light while still in the darkness."[3]

Today Christian believers stand in this long lineage and can confidently cry out "how long?" to this *same God* who has never ceased to bend his ear to his creation. The ancient prayers of the psalmists, uttered by Jesus, and prayed by the writers of the New Testament, can serve as both template and teacher as worshipers dialogue with God.

2. Eklund, *Practicing Lament*, 2.

3. Eklund, *Practicing Lament*, 40.

When Belief and Experience Collide

The confluence of the Mississippi and Missouri rivers is located very near to where I live in St. Louis, Missouri. Standing at the nearby lookout which extends out over the waters, one is quickly overtaken and made to feel small by the speed and power of the water as it flows past, churning into small whirlpools and white-capped waves as the two rivers collide. Anything thrown in is quickly swallowed up in the flow of the water and whisked downstream, never to be seen again. The collision between belief and experience can be equally, if not more powerful. Scott Ellington comments:

> When our beliefs collide with contradictory experiences, those experiences may be radically reinterpreted or even ignored entirely in order to sustain our beliefs. But there is a price to be paid for such alterations to experience, as cognitive dissonance grows between what we believe about God and the ways that we have access to him through experience. The belief that God hears and responds to prayers for healing when they are offered in faith, for example, is strained each time such prayers go unanswered. When the weight of contrary experiences grows sufficiently ponderous, basic beliefs will be re-evaluated and even changed.[4]

This collision of belief and experience is universal and cannot be avoided. For some, it is crippling, especially when it must be silenced or ignored because no safe space has been created where such questions of faith can be held in the worshiping community. As Ellington states, the price to be paid is enormous, and can lead to the abandonment of faith. This abandonment can be thorough and absolute, leading the believer to renounce the life of faith altogether, settling into ambivalence or outright disbelief. Alternatively, this abandonment can be inward, even while the outer person displays no signs of doubt, suffering, and the war within. Such decisions result from the human effort to self-protect, to make sense of the suffering, to maintain a place of belonging and a way to go forward. Sadly, the cost is often more than can be paid. The soul becomes

4. Ellington, *Risking Truth*, 13.

crushed under the load of doubt, the body breaks down with pain and disease, the mind grows depressed and distressed, and hope is lost. Dr. Marc Brackett, director of the Yale Center for Emotional Intelligence, has discovered, "Hurt feelings don't vanish on their own. They don't heal themselves. If we don't express our emotions, they pile up like a debt that will eventually come due."[5]

The Way of Christ

As with any human system, the Christian church has absorbed self-protecting behaviors, at times unwittingly; we cannot help but be products of the cultures in which we live. Triumphalism, nationalism, racism, sexism, individuality, beauty, strength, hurry, the "quick-fix" mentality, and the promotion of positive thinking to remove suffering have at times infiltrated church teaching and leadership. These philosophies have sadly influenced the message of the Gospel, watering it down and at times, making it unrecognizable.

But none of these are the way of Christ. The Old Testament prophet Isaiah described Christ as the man of sorrows, the one with no beauty or majesty, the despised and rejected lamb who was willingly slaughtered, who chose not to retaliate. Even in Isaiah's day, such a one was written off, as noted in Isa 53:4 (NRSV), "Yet we esteemed him stricken, struck down by God, and afflicted." But surely his suffering was the result of a lack of faith? Surely he was being judged for hidden sin? Isaiah continues in verses 7–9 (NRSV),

> He was oppressed, and he was afflicted,
> yet he did not open his mouth;
> like a lamb that is led to the slaughter,
> and like a sheep that before its shearers is silent,
> so he opened not his mouth.
> By a perversion of justice he was taken away.
> Who could have imagined his future?
> For he was cut off from the land of the living,
> Stricken for the transgression of my people.
> They made his grave with the wicked,

5. Brackett, *Permission to Feel*, 13.

and his tomb with the rich,
although he had done no violence,
and there was no deceit in his mouth.

The suffering way of the Lamb of God is the way to which we are called. We must reexamine the complex emotions of Christ, and acknowledge that he, too, possessed difficult and seemingly "negative" emotions. Only by reframing our understanding of Christ's pain, can we embrace and begin to understand our own, and in turn offer a safe place to hold the pain of others.

The Transformative Role of Suffering in Community

The New Testament epistles contain multiple admonitions to the first-century church and to believers throughout history, to rejoice as they remember the saving work of Christ (Rom 5:2–3, 12:12; Phil 3:1, 4:4; 1 Thess 5:16; 1 Pet 1:8). Indeed, believers have always had reason to rejoice as they considered Christ's triumphal resurrection. However, in his letter to the Philippian church, Paul shared a message which was countercultural in his day and remains so in the current culture. In chapter 3, which begins with the simple command to rejoice, Paul calls believers to not only share in the triumph of Christ, but also to share "his sufferings," all in an effort to know him (Phil 3:10 NRSV). To know Christ is to know a "man of suffering and acquainted with infirmity," as foretold in Isaiah's prophecy (Isa 53:3 NRSV).

A follower of Christ desires to share the message of Christ's triumph, to share the hope of healing, provision, and redemption. Offering the hope of Christ's salvific work in a world torn by war, violence, racism, disease, drug addiction, and economic decline that touches individuals and families every day is indeed the mission of the church (1 Cor 5:19). However, at times, the efforts of believers to share the hope of Christ seems to leave little if any room for "negative" emotional expressions in daily life, much less in corporate worship. Perhaps this fear is rooted in the belief that they will detract from the saving message of the gospel, or at least that they will appear to be failing as faithful believers.

Confusing faith with "positive thinking," Christians often struggle with the words of the psalmists and other biblical authors, confused by their raw, honest questions directed to Yahweh. For the psalmists, the clearest demonstration of faith was their appeal to "the right hand of the Most High" (Ps 77:10 NRSV), in an effort to "remind" Yahweh of his covenant promises to his people. The dialogical nature of Israel's relationship with Yahweh resulted in this kind of open, honest, and at times strikingly harsh speech. However, the psalmists relied on the relationship with Yahweh established generations before them, and expressed their complaints, fully trusting that they would be received, and that Yahweh would act based on historical precedent. Indeed, the loss of Yahweh's presence and his faithful provision left the psalmists sick, dejected, depressed, and in distress. David and the other psalmists seemed clearly convinced that these honest expressions of their struggles held the same value in worship to Yahweh as their prayers in the psalms of praise and thanksgiving.

If worship of the one God is to be formative and transformative for the worshiper, as both Old and New Testaments affirm (Isa 6:1–9; Rom 12:9–21), then worship must begin from a place of honesty. It seems to follow from this that the corporate worship service must be sensitively crafted to provide soul care for those who weep as well as those who rejoice.

The increased attention in the last decade to the place of lament in corporate worship demonstrates an increased understanding of the need for authenticity in emotional expression. Lament practices in corporate worship not only give place to individual expression, but also educate and equip believers to be aware of and respond to the cries of brokenness and suffering in their communities and across the globe, and to continue Christ's work of reconciliation in the world. Such practices are needed, not just during times of national or global crisis, but in the weekly corporate worship service, addressing the needs of individuals and the congregation as a whole. The Psalms must serve as both template and teacher if believers are to understand honest and authentic emotional expressions, and value their demonstrations of faith-filled dialogue between God and worshipers. These songs and prayers served both as a reminder of Yahweh's faithfulness in the past and called him to action in the individual and corporate life of Israel; their message continues to be relevant today.

This study addresses the need for balanced soul care in Christian worship with specific attention to the Psalms and other biblical models for lament, in the context of two overarching questions: (1) how do believers worship faithfully while holding in tension eschatological hope and clear and present suffering? and (2) how can the liturgy serve as a means of balanced soul care for all congregants, whatever the emotional state of each worshiper?

A Multi-Disciplinary Approach

Increasingly, scholars from a wide range of fields have begun to look through their unique lenses and consider the connection between suffering and the Christian life. These connections have made clearer the ways in which portions of Scripture such as the psalms of lament may serve as both a template and teacher for modern believers. If one considers the multi-dimensional nature of worship and the myriad ways in which it touches and transforms believers, any study of corporate worship cannot stand whole and balanced without the contribution of multiple disciplines. Given that human beings are complex and holistic beings, and that suffering always eventually affects a person wholly, the approach to addressing it cannot be one-dimensional.

Scholars of biblical and practical theology have especially focused on the psalms of lament and imprecation, as well as Jesus' own use of these prayers as reflected in the New Testament. Such work brings a depth of insight and understanding, and thus enables believers to engage and apply these models to daily living. Old Testament scholars such as Walter Brueggemann, Claus Westermann, John Goldingay, and Patrick D. Miller laid the foundation for this invaluable work, giving those in other fields a solid and indispensable biblical foundation on which to build. Familiarity with the ways in which suffering is framed in the Old Testament can give believers a clearer understanding of its intertextual appearances in the New Testament.

In addition to biblical and practical theology, the contributions of those in the fields of psychology, social work, and pastoral care *must* be drawn from and incorporated into the planning of corporate worship that addresses human suffering. The gifts of believers who work in these fields have been relegated for far too long to the small group, support group, and private counseling session. Individuals educated in these areas of soul care have unique insight into the way suffering disrupts and cripples the ability of human beings to function in healthy ways. Using such expertise to thoughtfully and sensitively craft the worship service can help equip pastors and worship leaders to order corporate worship in a way which cares for both individuals and the community in times of suffering.

Drawing from these and other disciplines, I will propose a framework within which a space for suffering can be furnished with thoughtful practices and sensitive responses that offer a safe space into which the hurting can come and begin the slow process of rebuilding.

Scope of the Study

Perhaps the greatest gift of the psalms of lament is their ability to allow worshipers to stand in a place free of shame. It is astonishing how freely the composers of these ancient songs expressed their feelings and emotions about life, loss, suffering, and their enemies. Careful reading of the lament and imprecatory psalms reveals a level of transparency that is almost always absent in modern corporate worship:

> I call to you, God, because I'm sure of an answer.
> So—answer! bend your ear! listen sharp!
> Paint grace-graffiti on the fences;
> take in your frightened children who
> are running from the neighborhood bullies
> straight to you.

Up, God: beard them! break them!
By your sword, free me from their clutches;
Barehanded, God, break these mortals,
these flat-earth people who can't think beyond today.
(Ps 17:6–7, 13–14, MSG)

If this psalmist felt shame about his anger, or fear about how God might respond, it is not indicated here. Instead of speaking what they thought God wanted to hear in order to be accepted, or to avoid feelings of shame and rejection, the psalmists demonstrated the singular essential ingredient necessary for dialogue with God: vulnerability.

The gift of the Psalms, therefore, is the way they redefine prayer and give new and authentic language to our current culture which teaches people to hide, to avoid expressions of weakness, sadness, depression, anger, and other so-called "negative" emotions—to be anything but vulnerable. An examination of the ways in which shame paralyzes people, rendering them incapable of allowing any glimpse of brokenness, is vital if corporate worship is to do its transformative work. Additionally, the hard work of examining the effects of shame on the church as a whole, and what is often its inability to admit or show weakness, is work that must be done if the church is to provide a safe space to stand and a soft place for the hurting to fall.

In order for believers and church leadership to not only see the value of shared expressions of suffering, but also weave them into corporate worship, a biblical foundation must be laid. While the Old Testament holds multiple examples of human and divine suffering, I will focus primarily on the psalms of lament and imprecation due to their use throughout the history of worship, beginning with ancient Israel and into the early centuries of the church. Next, I will explore Jesus' own use of the psalms throughout his ministry, and especially in his prayers. Such an examination gives believers a pattern for praying the psalms and also permission to use these plainspoken and honest expressions as template and teacher for individual and corporate prayers.

The following chapter will consist of an overview of the use of the Psalms by such biblical writers as Paul, Peter, and John in the Revelation. While the ethos of the psalms of lament echoed throughout the whole of the New Testament, these writers in particular demonstrate a straightforward and at times verbatim use of their worship language. Additionally, I will examine Jesus' use of the language of the Psalms in his teachings, particularly in the parables. This will demonstrate that beginning with Jesus, and throughout the New Testament, early Jewish converts to Christianity knew the psalms intimately and used them in corporate song, prayer, and teaching.

After laying a biblical foundation, I will examine modern corporate worship in light of the implications for soul care. What are modern believers to make of the wash of lament that literally opens and closes the biblical canon? From Abel's blood crying out from the earth to the martyrs in the Revelation, and everywhere in between, expressions of suffering pervade the biblical text. This undeniable element of Scripture, therefore, cannot be eliminated from corporate worship practices if believers are to live the whole and abundant life Christ promised (John 10:10). In light of this, I will examine six undergirding principles which ground corporate soul care practices:

1. The Psalms as God's "casebook" for soul care.

2. Worship is not pain denial.[6]

3. Worship is *dialogical* and *relational.*

4. Worship is ultimately communal.

5. Lament fuels authentic praise.

6. Lament has an eschatological dimension.

Examination of these six practices will be followed by three undergirding principles that allow believers to hold in tension the triumph of Christ's resurrection and the clear and present suffering

---

6. J. Runck, personal conversation, April 12, 2014.

in which they live individually, corporately, and globally in a world "destined for glory yet still unredeemed."[7]

Building on these implications, I will examine the fruits of lament. We do not implement services of lament simply to have a good cry or to vent anger and frustration, but because we know that in so doing, we are being formed more and more into the image of Christ, the "man of suffering" (Isa 53:3 NRSV). The fruits of lament call us into deeper, more authentic community with God and others. Greater intimacy, in turn, fosters the work of genuine compassion as we recognize our pain in the hearts of others. Lament also bears the invaluable fruit of hope as we join together to sit in the tension of present suffering and the promise of Christ's return when all things will be made new and every tear will be wiped away.

In conclusion, I will examine case studies from musical artists, visual artists, and works of literature which demonstrate the need for such expressions, both corporately and personally. These case studies will demonstrate that the human need to express suffering, and to support others in their time of need is as fundamental to human existence as the very air we breathe. Additionally, these case studies will demonstrate that healing and the ability to move forward can only come when suffering is voiced and shared, much as the psalmists have demonstrated.

It is my hope that in examining the widespread theme of lament throughout Scripture, and especially in the life of Christ, believers and students of theology will find in it cause to rejoice. The presence of lament in Scripture gives believers a reason to rejoice. Knowing that our suffering is felt and known by God, who chose not to remove himself from our pain, but instead chose to enter into it, gives believers permission to unashamedly bring these difficult expressions into his presence. In so doing we are reminded that the day will come when every tear will be wiped away, and our singular emotion will be the joy felt in his presence. Until that time, we mourn, we struggle, we pray, and we trust.

7. Black, "Persistence of the Wounds," 53.

2

Suffering and Lament in the Book of Psalms

The very presence of such prayers in Scripture is a witness to his understanding. He knows how [we] speak when [we] are desperate.

—DEREK KIDNER, *PSALMS*

IN ANY DISCUSSION OF biblical lament, the Psalms play a central role. Biblical scholars and theologians have recognized and devoted time and space to the precedents for corporate lament practices found in the Psalms as early as Hermann Gunkel's 1967 form-critical analysis, *The Psalms*, Klaus Westermann's *Praise and Lament in the Psalms* published in 1981, and Walter Brueggemann's 1984 article "The Costly Loss of Lament." Scholars of worship and liturgy have only more recently begun to understand with some consistency the importance of lament, exploring the nature and need to cultivate these practices within the last decade. In order to understand the need for and place of lament in corporate worship, one must first look to precedents and models found in Scripture.

In this chapter I present a discussion of the language and theology of lament as found in the Old Testament. The goal is not to develop a new theology of suffering, but rather to examine these theologies of suffering, using them as models for the contemporary context. In addition, I will explore J. L. Austin's "speech act theory" as it has been applied to the Psalms, resulting in a broadened understanding of the dialogical nature of Israel's worship practices.

THEOLOGY AND LANGUAGE
OF BIBLICAL LAMENT

The cries of lament across the biblical canon, and particularly in the Old Testament, demonstrate the centrality of such language in the prayer life of God's people. Though mostly found in Job, Psalms, Lamentations, and Jeremiah, the cry of the sufferer is heard consistently across the biblical canon, such as in Jacob's cry of fear at the thought of facing his brother, Esau (Gen 32:9–12); Hannah's agonizing plea to bear a child (1 Sam 1); Habakkuk's prayer of protest, with its richly complex issues of theodicy (Hab 2); Jesus' cry of dereliction from the cross (Mark 15:34); Paul's plea for God to remove the "thorn" in his flesh (2 Cor 12:7–8); and the cry of the martyrs in the Revelation (Rev 6:9–11). These prayers of lament demonstrate the consistency of such expressions across the biblical canon, serving as examples for us today.

The relationship between Israel and Yahweh in the Old Testament was dialogical in nature, involving individuals or the community as a whole. Foundational to this relationship is the faithfulness and *hesed*, or "steadfast love," of Yahweh, a central part of God's character to which the people of the Old Testament returned and upon which they consistently relied. At the heart of this relationship is the covenant sworn between Yahweh and Israel, one in which each party was bound by a loyal commitment (Exod 19, 24). Indeed, as the people broke the covenant, God meted out judgment, punishing the people for their sin (e.g., 2 Kgs 17:7–8; Jer 32:26–33; Ps 78:59–62). Yet even with judgment looming, he *spoke* to his people through the prophets, and continued to hear their repentant cries for deliverance. Israel's prayer, therefore, was contingent upon the state of the covenant. When the covenant was functioning well, dialogue was largely based in praise and thanksgiving; when broken, the offended partner would, in the words of Walter Brueggemann, "attempt to reach across the breach" in order to restore covenantal equilibrium.[1]

In both the prose and poetic prayers of lament in the Old Testament, the intimacy of the divine covenant relationship is readily found in the forms of address with which the people called on Yahweh. Often overlooked by modern readers, the address typically found at the beginning and again at the conclusion of Old Testament prayers further reinforces the nation's reliance on Yahweh's covenant faithfulness, while adding urgency to the petition or complaint.[2] Addresses such as "O God" or "O Lord" (e.g., Gen 15:1–6; Exod 5:22–23; Num 14:13–19; Jer 32:16–25) are most commonly found. Cries of "Most high God," or "the Holy One of Israel" are also often found in the lament psalms, serving as a reminder to either individuals or the community that Yahweh's power and might surpass the dire situation and he is able to redeem.

Even more personal than the above addresses are the appeals of "my God" (Ps 22:1 NRSV), "You are my God" (Ps 140:6 NRSV), or "our God" (2 Chron 14:11 NRSV). These highly personal forms of address indicate the central element of trust on which the covenant with Yahweh was built.[3] To appeal to him as "my God" or "our God" gives even greater weight to the closeness of the covenantal relationship.[4] This claim indicates the depth and breadth of not only the psalmist's relationship with Yahweh, but also the

1. Brueggemann, *Reverberations of Faith*, 147.

2. Miller, *They Cried to the Lord*, 58.

3. Miller, *They Cried to the Lord*, 59.

4. Although not a prayer of lament, Ps 18 is a prime example of the use of the personal "my," as it uses this pronoun thirteen times throughout the course of this single psalm. Attributed to David, this prayer of thanksgiving celebrates many facets of God's character in the psalmist's mind: my shield, my rock, my salvation, etc. Miller notes that the person praying sees God as *pro me* as he builds on these assertions and divine character traits. Miller, *They Cried to the Lord*, 60.

Suffering and Lament in the Book of Psalms

relationship with him throughout time, beginning with the Abrahamic covenant of Gen 15. The psalmist likely viewed this address
as a means to "motivate" Yahweh and remind him of his reputation
for trustworthiness among the nations besides Israel.[5]

The personal nature of the address is grounded in remembrance of God's soteriological acts, which are reflected in his dialogical relationship with Israel.[6] God's saving acts found in the Old
Testament are foundational to the story of Israel and are often the
result of the cry "out of the depths" from the people, a cry rooted
in covenant. Indeed, we cannot engage a theology of the Old Testament without regarding as foundational the saving acts of Yahweh
in response to the cry of his people. This engagement requires that
we see lament as a central element not only in the history of Israel,
but also in an understanding of God as a relational being. Claus
Westermann notes that much of Western contemporary theology
has been characterized by "objective thinking about God," which is
in direct opposition to the Old Testament presentation of a subjective God who is "characterized by dialogical thinking," a God who
did not fail to respond to the emotional cries of his people.[7]

Given the centrality of lament to the relationship between
Israel and Yahweh in Old Testament theology, one can conclude
that expressions of suffering are necessary and even expected by
God. Westermann comments:

> In both the Old and New Testaments the lament is a very
> natural part of human life; in the Psalter it is an impor-
> tant and inescapable component of worship and of the
> language of worship. In the Old Testament there is not a
> single line which would forbid the lamentation or which
> would express the idea that lamentation had no place in
> a healthy and good relationship with God.[8]

5. Brueggemann, *Reverberations of Faith*, 148. See for example Ps 79:10 in
which the psalmist asks, "Why should the nations say, 'Where is their God?'
Let the avenging of the outpoured blood of your servants be known among the
nations before our eyes!"

6. Westermann, "Role of Lament," 22.

7. Westermann, "Role of Lament," 22.

8. Westermann, "Role of Lament," 25.

Because Israel understood this freedom of expression to Yahweh, suffering and its accompanying emotions were understood by men and women of the Old Testament as an offering of worship as valued as praise and thanksgiving.[9] Furthermore, the expression and processing of these emotions in the presence of Yahweh served a two-fold purpose: (1) an act of trust grounded in the historical covenantal relationship, and (2) the expression of suffering and grief to one who had the power to intervene so that evil would not be accepted as the norm.[10]

The psalmist's ability to dialogue freely with Yahweh across the spectrum of emotions and life experiences was grounded in both his trust in Yahweh's faithfulness and its outgrowth, the gift of life itself. Brueggemann and Bellinger note that Yahweh's "fidelity" was the foundation upon which the psalmist's relationship with him was built.[11] From the Abrahamic covenant of Gen 15 onward, the gift of life given to Israel was embraced as Yahweh's promise to his people. If Israel would love and obey his laws, the promises of steadfast love, mercy, grace, righteousness, and justice would be the promised result. Brueggemann and Bellinger comment that this obedience on the part of God's people "is a full existence of trust in and loyalty to a covenant partner, trust and loyalty that are embodied in obedience to instructions but that bespeak an interpersonal, interactive communion, and not simply compliance with a set of rules."[12]

9. Author and pastor Tim Keller comments, "Sociologists and anthropologists have analyzed and compared the various ways that cultures train its members for grief, pain, and loss. And when this comparison is done, it is often noted that our own contemporary secular, Western culture is one of the weakest, and worst in history at doing so." Keller goes on to note that most societies work to provide a "discourse," or means to make sense of suffering. He cites the vastly varied responses to the Newtown, Connecticut school shootings in December 2012, and how the vastly varied responses to newspaper articles on the massacre demonstrated the lack of emotional tools for processing such tragedy, resulting in the need to turn to other cultures and religions (Hindu, Buddhist, Confucianist, classical Greek, and Christian) for answers. Tim Keller, *Walking with God through Pain and Suffering*, 14–15.

10. McCann, *Theological Introduction to the Book of Psalms*, 118.

11. Brueggemann and Bellinger, *Psalms*, 520.

12. Brueggemann and Bellinger, *Psalms*, 520.

THEOLOGY OF SUFFERING IN THE PSALMS

Much of the theology of suffering in the Old Testament can be said to be embodied in psalms of lament, for it is there that many of the most intense and personal expressions of suffering are found. Voiced primarily from the human perspective, unlike divine laments recorded elsewhere in Scripture, the psalms of lament are pleas for deliverance, healing, and/or forgiveness with a holistic focus that brings the whole person, with all accompanying emotions, before God.[13] What is important to all the various perspectives is the need to bring the suffering to speech. The articulation of grief to Yahweh is a safe place to verbally process the suffering and avoid the probability of hopelessness that would be brought on by silence or isolation.[14] The psalmists understood that neither "processing (for the hurting) nor understanding (for the empathizing)" could take place until grief had been expressed in speech.[15] The types of laments vary and include cries of complaint, pleas, confessions of guilt, or acts of protest. Regardless of the type, the unifying factors among these laments are the covenantal relationship and the realization that deliverance can come from Yahweh alone.

This sense of safety in articulating suffering is grounded in the covenantal commitment between Yahweh and his people and serves as the foundation upon which the lament is built. While cries such as "How long, O Lord?" might appear to carry connotations

13. Pierce, *Enthroned on Our Praise*, 244.

14. Brueggemann, *Hope within History*, 88. Bruggemann references Ps 39, in which the psalmist realizes the cost of guarding and silencing his suffering, and ultimately chooses to speak out. Brueggemann states, "Speech breaks the despair. The speech out of despair moves toward and addresses God, the subject of hope. As silence leads to hopelessness, so speech invites the God of all hope to be present." Brueggemann, *Hope within History*, 39. See also Brueggemann, *Israel's Praise*, 142.

15. Peterman and Schmutzer, "Grammar of Suffering," 23. The authors note the need to "read and translate" what they have called the various "grammars" of suffering such as speech, visual art, dance, music, or even silence. For further discussion on the role of music in processing and expressing suffering, see William Dyrness, "Prophesy to these Dry Bones: The Artist's Role in Healing the Earth," in Goroncy *Tikkun Olam*, 21–36.

of mistrust, they are acts of great faith in that they appeal to Yahweh's record of covenant faithfulness, steadfast love, and mercy, and according to John Eaton, are "grounded upon the certainty of the divine-human relationship."[16] Scott Ellington explores the connection between lament and covenant relationship more closely:

> Biblical lament, while it does include tears, pleas, complaints and protests, is something more. It is the experience of loss suffered within the context of *relatedness*. A relationship of trust, intimacy, and love is a necessary precondition for genuine lament. When the biblical writers lament, they do so from within the context of a foundational relationship that binds together the individual with members of the community of faith and that community with their God.[17]

Not only were the psalmists appealing to Yahweh based upon his faithfulness in their individual lives, but also in the entire history of Israel. This appeal to God's record of faithfulness is demonstrated in passages such as Ps 77:9–12 (NRSV):

> 9 Has God forgotten to be gracious?
>   Has he in anger shut up his
>   compassion?"
> 10 And I say, "It is my grief
>   that the right hand of the Most
>   High has changed."
> 11 I will call to mind the deeds
>   of the LORD;
>   I will remember your
>   wonders of old.
> 12 I will meditate on all your work,
>   And must on your mighty deeds.

In the words of Samuel Balentine, the biblical laments drew the suffering "into the orbit of Yahweh's concern" and thus

---

16. Eaton, *Psalms*, 235.

17. Ellington, *Risking Truth*, 7, emphasis original.

constituted a clear act of trust, serving to strengthen and deepen the covenantal relationship.[18]

The covenantal nature of the expressions found in the Psalms brings unique insight into the ways and means of processing emotions in ancient Israel. For the psalmists and other Old Testament figures, it was natural to process and pray all emotions in the presence of Yahweh. Tim Keller distinguishes between expressions of suffering in the Psalms and modern approaches for processing feelings. Keller notes that religion often teaches people to either "deny their feelings" or to be "under-awed" by feelings, while contemporary secular society often encourages individuals to "vent feelings" and even to be "over-awed" by them.[19] The psalms offer what Keller terms a "Gospel third way" for processing emotions: rather than deny or vent emotions, believers are to *pray* the particular emotion to God.[20] Keller states:

> The Psalms say it is very dangerous to deny your feelings or vent your feelings, to either stuff your feelings or bow down to your feelings. The Psalms tell us we are supposed to pray our feelings, not just pray about our feelings. [We are] to actually take them before God and pour them out in a pre-reflective way, and process them in the presence of God, in the light of who he is and who we are, in the light of the realities that come to us and bear down on us as we are in his presence.[21]

These unfiltered outpourings across the emotional spectrum found in the Psalms constitute what Keller has termed "God's case book," God's resource given to believers as a means for further developing both the individual and corporate relationship with him.[22]

---

18. Balentine, *Prayer in the Hebrew Bible*, 263. See also Brueggemann, *Reverberations of Faith*, 202.

19. Keller, "Praying Your Tears."

20. Keller, "Praying Your Tears."

21. Keller, "Praying Your Guilt."

22. Keller, "Praying Your Tears."

Orientation, Disorientation, and Reorientation in the Psalms

The richness of the Psalms is partly found in the diversity of expressions across the emotional spectrum explored. Throughout much of the twentieth century, biblical scholars such as Gunkel, Mowinckel, Mays, McCann, and Westermann have developed typologies or categorizations of the psalms.[23] While neat categories might facilitate use and application of individual psalms, much recent psalm scholarship commends canonical reading of the Psalter as a means of mining fresh insights into thematic unity in the Psalms, both between the five scribally edited books of the Psalter, and into the overall trajectory of the book. N. T. Wright advocates enthusiastically for reading the book of Psalms as a whole, contending the reader should travel through the Psalter, experiencing the ebb and flow from praise to lament and the many emotions in between, in order to understand their interrelatedness in the worship life of Israel and their application to current worship practices.[24] Indeed, as we read through the Psalter, the dynamic flow between the psalms of praise and lament gives evidence of the rich dialogical nature of Israel's relationship with Yahweh. At the heart of this dynamic relational flow is the assertion that "the LORD reigns" and the unmovable truth that all of life functions around this covenantal promise, according to psalm scholar James Mays.[25]

23. For example, Brueggemann, *Message of the Psalms*; Mays, *Lord Reigns*; McCann, *Theological Introduction to the Psalms*; Westermann, *Praise and Lament in the Psalms*.

24. On the ebb and flow of the Psalms, N. T. Wright comments, "The Psalms, I want to suggest here, are songs and poems that help us not just to *understand* this most ancient and relevant worldview [of God's view of time, space, and matter], but actually to *inhabit* and *celebrate* it—this worldview in which, contrary to most modern assumptions, God's time and ours overlap and intersect, God's space and ours overlap and interlock, and even (this is the really startling one, of course) the sheer material world of God's creation is infused, suffused, and flooded with God's own life and love and glory. The Psalms will indeed help us to understand all of this." Wright, *Case for the Psalms*, 22.

25. Mays, *Psalms*, 31.

Mays notes further, "The prayers of the people of God are based on the confidence that the proclamation is true."[26] All of ancient Israel's life revolved around this central truth.

When we consider that the psalmists filtered life through the lens of Yahweh's unquestionable reign and abiding presence, our understanding of the psalms of lament is reshaped, allowing greater understanding of the sometimes raw and anguished expressions found there. When this proclamation was in conflict with the psalmists' lived experience, they lamented in an effort to bring reality into alignment with their belief in Yahweh's rule and reign. That life had become unbalanced or untethered from the security of his presence was unacceptable and even unbearable to the psalmists. In the cry of lament, Brueggemann notes, "God is summoned relentlessly into the now," in an effort to restore equilibrium and to reaffirm to the psalmist the fact of Yahweh's reign.[27] Indeed, these multivalent, faith-filled expressions of suffering were brought before the one and only source of relief and restoration known in the history of Israel: Yahweh himself.

This tension between belief and experience is key to understanding the psalms of lament; Scott Ellington describes it as a collision of these two truths.[28] Belief, according to Ellington, is that which we reason to be true about God, the way in which we define the relationship with him in times of order and calm.[29] Conversely, experience is more difficult to define, "less tidy," and often does not fit perfectly with our beliefs.[30] Belief—that which is clear "on paper"—is often challenged when we attempt to incorporate it into actual experience. For instance, how do we respond when prayers for healing are offered, only to be met with the perceived silence of God? When met with the repeated or protracted challenges of painful experience, our beliefs can be reexamined or even changed

26. Mays, *Psalms*, 31.

27. Brueggemann, *Israel's Praise*, 137.

28. Ellington, *Risking Truth*, 12.

29. Ellington, *Risking Truth*, 12.

30. Ellington, *Risking Truth*, 12.

in order to ease the tension.[31] Ellington explains the place of lament within this tension:

> The prayer of lament arises from an experience that challenges belief: a tragic event is followed by God's subsequent lack of response to prayer, thus raising questions and doubts about the nature of God's relationship with his people. Lament places a strong affirmation of belief, that God is a God who hears and delivers, over against an experience of God's silence and hiddenness in times of need.[32]

The biblical prayers of lament were the result of the working out of this tension, of the wrestling between the limited understanding of humanity and the all-encompassing wisdom and sovereignty of Yahweh, evidenced in his record and promise of faithfulness to his people.

Central to Walter Brueggemann's theology of the Psalms, and particularly this tension in the lament psalms, is the "cycle" or movement he traces from the psalmist's established belief in God, or orientation, into an experience of disequilibrium, or disorientation, and ultimately to a state of new orientation.[33] Brueggemann is careful to note that the movement through these stages is not always linear or a "once-for-all experience," because the unpredictable nature of life prevents such certainty.[34] Furthermore, he explains that while some psalms of lament complete the entire cycle, others may be partial, representative of a single stage of the cycle. Regardless of the configuration within a given psalm or within the life of a Christian believer, Brueggemann maintains that the life of faith for God's people regularly moves between the stages of disorientation and new orientation.[35] The new orientation becomes common or even mundane before being interrupted by

31. Ellington, *Risking Truth*, 14.
32. Ellington, *Risking Truth*, 14.
33. Brueggemann, *Message of the Psalms*, 19.
34. Brueggemann, *Message of the Psalms*, 22.
35. Brueggemann, *Message of the Psalms*, 22.

disorientation, beginning the cycle anew. What follows is a brief examination of the three stages of Brueggemann's typology.

Orientation

The psalms of orientation present a sense of equilibrium and settled peace. Called psalms or "hymns" of praise, these psalms express thanksgiving, confidence, or remembrance of Yahweh's faithfulness in the history of Israel, or celebrate his royal reign and reputation as a mighty warrior and conqueror of Israel's enemies.[36] In a state of orientation, there is no sense of threat, no need for fear, and instead an abiding sense of God's unquestionable faithfulness. Brueggemann describes orientation as "a state of God's faithfulness and goodness... experienced as generosity, continuity, and regularity."[37]

It is important to note that the state of orientation is not a world devoid of the awareness of suffering; as noted, orientation was once experienced as "new orientation," or the state of being *after* a season of disorientation. Instead, Brueggemann explains this as a season lived underneath the "canopy of certitude."[38] He continues by noting that this certitude brings with it a "givenness to be relied upon," a remembrance of transitions *from* disorientation *into* new orientation, and the confidence that this will once again be the case.[39] Although the immediate conclusion could

36. Nowell, *Pleading, Cursing, Praising*, 87. Also see the seminal work by Westermann on the use of the word "hymn" in describing certain psalms of praise. Westermann builds on the work of Gunkel and Mowinckel in his attempt to situate the hymn of praise within the cultic worship of Israel. See Westermann, *Praise and Lament*, 11–30.

37. Brueggemann, *Message of the Psalms*, 26.

38. Brueggemann, *Message of the Psalms*, 27.

39. Brueggemann, *Message of the Psalms*, 27. Interestingly, Brueggemann comments that such a "canopy of certitude" can easily become a form of social control: "But there are times when such psalms must be used carefully or with a knowing qualification. . . . Then we must always ask whose interest is reflected and served by such psalms and by their use." The unhealthy result of the insistent use of such psalms to the exclusion of the laments is that one could fall into a "system of obedience and rewards," or even inculcate believers with a fear of honest emotive expressions in corporate worship. The need to maintain

be that these psalms are only for use in times of perceived peace and safety, we must be careful not to overlook their eschatological function. We must note the presence of the "already-and-not-yet" in these psalms, which enables even the suffering to turn to them. The note of eschatological hope enables the orientation psalms to inspire both immediate and present confidence in Yahweh as well as a broader hope of transformation, which will lead to *"transformation and new creation."*[40]

Psalms of orientation are generally communal, as they often call others to join in the praise of Yahweh. Given that psalms of orientation were at some point expressions of new orientation, one can find upon careful examination a review or summary of a time of trouble from which the psalmist was delivered. The praise of Yahweh is the natural outgrowth of this deliverance, and its level of exuberance must match, or even outstrip, the intensity of the previous suffering as Mays points out.[41] An example of this call to corporate praise of Yahweh is found in Ps 145 (NRSV), which intensifies as it describes God's gracious oversight of mankind. Verses 8 and 9 describe Yahweh as "gracious," "merciful," and "slow to anger," and represent a recollection of an individual or corporate time of suffering and subsequent deliverance. Similarly, verses 14, 18, and 19 remind the congregation that Yahweh "upholds all who are falling, and raises up all who are bowed down," "is near to all who call on him," and "hears their cry and saves them." This psalm served as a kind of literary "altar" of remembrance, to borrow Brueggemann's phrase, to which the people could return in coming seasons of disorientation.[42]

---

a status quo of positive thinking (which is often substituted for biblical faith) could be the unfortunate result of the exclusive use of psalms of orientation.

40. Brueggemann, *Message of the Psalms*, 28, emphasis original.

41. Mays, *Psalms*, 24.

42. Brueggemann, *Message of the Psalms*, 28.

Disorientation

Entire psalms of disorientation, or psalms that contain segments of disorientation, comprise the largest category in the Psalter in Brueggemann's typology.[43] In addition to those generally known as psalms of lament or suffering, other categories or types include psalmic prayers of complaint, distress, or protest. Sixty-seven of the 150 psalms can thus be identified as some form of lament, with 49 being individual laments, and 18 representing laments of the community or entire nation of Israel.[44]

The psalms of lament, and other laments found regularly throughout the Old Testament, generally do not offer an explanation for suffering. As we will see in the forthcoming discussion, according to Peterman and Schmutzer, the Old Testament "recontextualizes" suffering by "placing it inside a dynamic of covenantal relationship."[45] In contrast to substitutionary suffering found in the New Testament, the Old Testament focuses more prominently on innocent suffering and issues of theodicy and the prosperity of the wicked.[46] Given the dialogical nature of Israel's relationship with Yahweh, there is an abiding expectation that God will vindicate Israel's suffering when they cry out to him (e.g., Ps 94:1–3; Isa 57:17–21; Hab 3:12–15).[47]

Although at first glance the psalms of disorientation may appear to be mostly individual in expression, they are imbued with a communal framework found in the recurring complaint regarding a sense of isolation brought on by the suffering, as noted in Ps 42:4 (NRSV): "These things I remember as I pour out my soul: how I

43. Nowell, *Pleading, Cursing, Praising,* 87.

44. Brueggemann and Bellinger, *Psalms,* 9–12. This text contains a helpful chart delineating all psalms into particular types. An alternate classification is noted by Peterman and Schmutzer who categorize the laments as follows: forty-two individual, sixteen corporate, nine that use some lament. Andrew Schmutzer, "Longing to Lament," in Peterman and Schmutzer, *Between Pain and Grace,* 107.

45. Peterman and Schmutzer, "Grammar of Suffering," 21, emphasis original.

46. Peterman and Schmutzer, "Grammar of Suffering," 27.

47. Peterman and Schmutzer, "Grammar of Suffering," 27.

went with the throng, and lead them in procession to the house of God with glad shouts and songs of thanksgiving, a multitude keeping festival." In essence, the movement from orientation to disorientation left the psalmist feeling marginalized and in isolation, no longer able to participate in key communal events of the corporate worship life of God's people. Requests and thanksgiving for oneself or others were most often offered *along with* the worshiping community at festivals, or in villages or families.[48] Goldingay explores this communal element:

> The story of Hannah suggests that even individual prayers may naturally take place at the sanctuary, though one may then pray them as an individual not in the context of the community's worship. Praying on your own is possible but is often a sign of things being wrong in some way. To have to pray on one's own is a sign of how needy one is, abandoned by or separated from other people. An aspect of the predicament out of which one then prays is the individual's isolation from the community.[49]

That such prayers would take place in isolation from others may intensify the focus of the prayer on the most pressing issue in need of resolution: the lack of community.[50]

48. Peterman and Schmutzer, "Grammar of Suffering," 27.

49. Goldingay, *Israel's Life*, 196.

50. Greenberg, *Biblical Prose Prayer*, 51. The connection between the psalmist's cry of dereliction, abandonment, and modern soul care is apparent. In writing on the goals of Christian soul care, Eric Johnson cites one goal of discourse as interpersonal relationship. As beings created and shaped in the image of God, believers are inherently dialogical beings. That Johnson states "Dialogue is fundamental to the life of persons" is not surprising (Johnson, *Foundations for Soul Care*, 14). Neither is it surprising, then, that the psalmists' principle cry was against the isolation experienced as a result of suffering. Johnson continues, "Christian soul care, according to this model, promotes relational communication through dialogue. God is a dialogue partner in the Christian healing of the soul, and we are always situated in the midst of a history and matrix of human conversations, one of which is that between counselor and counselee. Understood rightly—by faith—Christian soul care is always a *trialogue*, involving counselor, counselee, and the omnipresent God" (Johnson, *Foundations for Soul Care*, 15). The connections to corporate worship can be made given its communal nature.

Besides being marginalized from the immediate community, the psalmist also cries out against the alienation he feels from all generations of God's people before him. Ellington states, "That to which the psalmist appeals is far greater than the crisis of the moment or even the community that is physically present. The community of Israel shares in an enduring relationship of steadfast love with an eternal God."[51] The fact that this remembrance of and appeal to Yahweh's time-transcending love and faithfulness is found throughout the Psalter brings further weight and significance to its use by the psalmist. Indeed, specific psalms call the people to worship of Yahweh simply by reciting portions of Israel's history.[52] These psalms served as testimonies to Yahweh's faithfulness and helped to tether the psalmist to the larger sense of his or her place in the multi-generational community of Israel.[53]

That the psalmist *expected* Yahweh to save him is evident in the consistent appeal to his providential acts throughout the history of Israel as well as to the defining attributes of his character. In Moses' meeting with God on Mt. Sinai during which he received a second copy of the Ten Commandments, Yahweh described his defining attributes: "The LORD passed before him and proclaimed, 'The LORD, the LORD, a God merciful and gracious, slow to anger, and abounding in steadfast love and faithfulness'" (Exod 34:6 NRSV). It was to these very attributes the psalmists so often appealed, whether separately or in their entirety. Psalm 25:6 (NRSV) states, "Be mindful of your mercy, O LORD, and your steadfast love, for they have been from of old." Psalm 136 (NRSV), with its recurring interlinear refrain, "For his steadfast love endures forever," encapsulates the entire history of the world, from creation to the present, and Israel's story, all grounded in Yahweh's steadfast love. Psalm 86 (NRSV), quoted here in its entirety, situates within the cry for deliverance an appeal to the entire list of Yahweh's attributes:

---

51. Ellington, *Risking Truth*, 68.

52. See for example Pss 78, 105, 106, and 136.

53. Martin, "Book of Psalms and Pentecostal Worship," in Martin, *Toward a Pentecostal Theology of Worship*, 47–88.

Suffering, Soul Care, and Community

1 Incline your ear, O LORD,
  and answer me,
  for I am poor and needy.
2 Preserve my life, for I am
  devoted to you;
  save your servant who trusts in you.
3 You are my God; be gracious
  to me, O Lord,
  for to you do I cry all day long.
4 Gladden the soul of your servant,
  for to you, O Lord, I lift up my soul.
5 For you, O Lord, are good and forgiving,
  Abounding in steadfast love
  to all who call on you.
6 Give ear, O LORD, to my prayer;
  listen to my cry of supplication.
7 In the day of my trouble I call on you,
  for you will answer me.

8 There is none like you among
  the gods, O Lord,
  nor are there any works like yours.
9 All the nations you have
  made shall come
  and bow down before you, O Lord,
  and shall glorify your name.
10 For you are great and do
  wondrous things;
  you alone are God.
11 Teach me your way, O LORD,
  that I may walk in your truth;
  give me an undivided heart
  to revere your name.
12 I give thanks to you, O Lord my
  God, with my whole heart,
  and I will glorify your name forever.
13 For great is your steadfast
  love toward me;
  you have delivered my soul from
  the depths of Sheol.

14 O God, the insolent rise up against me;
a band of ruffians seeks my life
and they do not set you before them.
15 But you, O Lord, are a God
merciful and gracious,
slow to anger and abounding in
steadfast love and faithfulness.
16 Turn to me and be gracious to me;
give your strength to your servant;
save the child of your serving girl.
17 Show me a sign of your favor,
so that those who hate me may
see it and be put to shame,
because you, LORD, have helped
me and comforted me.

While verses 3, 5, 6, and 13 each reference at least one of Yahweh's defining attributes, verse 15 crescendos into a mighty climax of the full list.

Although this psalm begins as a complaint, it also contains a feature unique to the psalms of lament: what Brueggemann and Bellinger call the "motivational clause."[54] Verses 1, 2, 3, 4, and 7 contain the word "for," which introduces the reason the psalmist believes Yahweh should act on the psalmist's behalf: the psalmist is poor and needy, is devoted; the psalmist cries to the LORD all day, lifts up his soul to the LORD, for Yahweh answers. Verses 14 and 17 serve as further motivation for Yahweh to act since the adversaries, in their abuse of the psalmist, also bring disrespect and insult to Yahweh whom he serves.[55] Brueggemann and Bellinger explain what is at the heart of the psalm:

> Finally, in verse 17, this one who is steadfast, incomparable, and "God alone" is the God of all comfort, who will answer the prayer and act on behalf of the petitioner. Thus, all of the great claims made for YHWH now come down to the specificity of action for this lowly servant in

54. Brueggemann and Bellinger, *Psalms*, 372. See also Miller, *They Cried to the Lord*, 114–15.

55. Brueggemann and Bellinger, *Psalms*, 372.

need. Even this "child of a servant girl" does not doubt that the incomparable God can and will be attentive to this voice of need, hope, and faith. . . . The "I" of petition is taken with full seriousness, but the hope of the "I" is to have doxological lips that are fully occupied by the "thou" of power and fidelity. . . . It is no wonder, moreover, that the "I" knows and relies fully on this intimate and undoubted source of help and comfort.[56]

This psalm holds in perfect tension the legitimacy of complaint in the face of suffering alongside an unshakable reliance on and trust in Yahweh's covenantal commitment to him and the larger community of Israel. This is no impulsive, hasty, or "knee-jerk" expression of trust; rather, it is one grounded in the history of Yahweh's own well-known foundational promise of covenantal faithfulness and steadfast love.[57]

New Orientation

While the experience of disorientation is clearly expressed and processed in the book of Psalms, it is never, with the exception of Ps 88, where the psalmists remain. Brueggemann comments, "While the speaker may on occasion be left 'in the Pit,' (as in Ps 88), that is not the characteristic case. Most frequently the psalms stay with the experience to bring the speech to a *second decisive move*, from disorientation to new orientation."[58] As with disorientation, new orientation can account for a portion of a psalm of lament, or the entire psalm, in what is often categorized as psalms

---

56. Brueggemann and Bellinger, *Psalms*, 373.

57. Brueggemann and Bellinger link this confession of trust to the first answer of the Heidelberg Catechism: "Question: What is your only source of comfort and strength in this age and in the age to come? Answer: That I belong to my faithful Savior Jesus Christ." The authors comment, "The petition of this psalm and the affirmation of the catechism come to the same point: that I belong to my faithful Savior. No wonder the 'thou' of God prevails over the need of 'I.'" Brueggemann and Bellinger, *Psalms*, 374.

58. Brueggemann and Bellinger, *Psalms*, 123, emphasis added.

of thanksgiving or praise.[59] Although the most frequent movement found in the Psalms is from lament to praise, other patterns can be identified, including a move from praise to lament (Pss 3, 6, 13), from lament to praise with a return to lament (Pss 12, 28), or a vacillation between lament and praise.[60]

The turn from lament to praise (or new orientation) in individual psalms of lament has been a consistent point of interest for Old Testament scholars. Some argue that the turn was caused by a word from a prophet or priest, assuring the psalmist's prayers were heard and the deliverance sought has been granted.[61] Other scholars argue that the praise found at the conclusion of the psalm was later combined with the initial lament, after the sought-for deliverance came (Pss 3, 28, 31).[62] In this case, whether a day or many years have passed since the suffering was experienced, the psalmist is recalling the disorientation and the subsequent deliverance that resulted in new orientation.[63] Brueggemann comments that these recollections, or "rush of positive responses" such as thanksgiving and amazement, find their way into the original prayer of lament.[64] Some explain the "turn" from lament to praise as a "psychological shift," resulting in an expression of confidence that Yahweh *will* grant the deliverance needed, or that forgiveness for sin committed

---

59. Brueggemann and Bellinger, *Psalms*, 123.

60. Villanueva, *"Uncertainty of a Hearing,"* 121, cited in Schmutzer and Howard, *Psalms*, 151.

61. Brueggemann and Bellinger, *Psalms*, 50. See also Daniel Estes, "The Transformation of Pain into Praise," in Schmutzer and Howard, *Psalms*, 152.

62. Daniel Estes, "The Transformation of Pain into Praise," in Schmutzer and Howard, *Psalms*, 151–64.

63. Peterman and Schmutzer note that the laments can even switch tenses between the past and the present: "Laments do not capture the when of distress; rather, they highlight the *what* of personal suffering now felt throughout the psalmist's relational ecosystem." Considering this lack of reference to the specific time of the suffering, it is logical to conclude that the "turn" to new orientation/praise could have come at a variety of times after the suffering. See Schmutzer, "Longing to Lament: Returning to the Language of Suffering," in Peterman and Schmutzer, *Between Pain and Grace*, 103–30.

64. Brueggemann, *Spirituality of the Psalms*, 11.

will be granted (Pss 9, 71, 77).[65] Daniel Estes states, "By uttering the divine name, he could be sure that help was on the way to meet his need. . . . Having made this vow and anticipating God's resultant intervention in his life, the psalmist is liberated from his pain to praise God."[66] Scholars such as Leann Snow Flesher believe the "turn" can be best understood through a combination of the prophetic word or expression of confidence, depending on the particular psalmist.[67]

Understanding the "turn" in the lament psalm as a new orientation requires us to reconsider whole psalms of praise, thanksgiving, and celebration as a possible response to a period of corporate or individual lament.[68] Brueggemann has written that praise typically arose in the life of Israel after a time of suffering, and it would be consistent to draw a similar conclusion when considering the individual lament psalms.[69] In light of this ultimate transition to praise, one can more easily understand Westermann's view of a "continuum" along which all psalmic prayers, both corporate and individual, are situated.[70] If all prayers found in the Psalms are found along this continuum, as Westermann believes, then all are connected to both praise and lament.[71] He states,

> There is no petition [in the Psalms], no pleading from the depths, that did not move at least one step (in looking back to God's earlier saving activity or in confession of confidence) on the road to praise. But there is also no praise that was fully separated from the experience of

65. Daniel Estes, "The Transformation of Pain into Praise," in Schmutzer and Howard, *Psalms*, 151–64.

66. Daniel Estes, "The Transformation of Pain into Praise," in Schmutzer and Howard, *Psalms*, 151–64.

67. Flesher, "Rapid Change of Mood," in Foster and Howard, *My Words are Lovely*, 35–45.

68. Flesher, "Rapid Change of Mood," in Foster and Howard, *My Words are Lovely*, 35–45.

69. Brueggemann, *Israel's Praise*, 140.

70. Westermann, *Praise and Lament*, 74–75.

71. Westermann, *Praise and Lament*, 75.

God's wonderful intervention in time of need, none that
had become a mere stereotyped liturgy.[72]

One can see that the remembrance of Yahweh's salvific actions to earlier generations, or the promise of salvation to come,
propelled the psalmists along the continuum, moving them ever
closer to praise as suffering resolved into new orientation.[73]

It is most important to understand that the transition from
disorientation to new orientation was not a return to life as experienced *before* the suffering. Considering this transformation, it is
important to label this final stage of the "cycle" *new orientation*, as
opposed to *reorientation*, given the transformative nature of suffering. Not only is the source of the suffering relieved, changed, or
removed, but the psalmist's view of Yahweh, himself, the community, and the source of suffering itself is transformed. This transformation is noted in Ps 73 (NRSV), as the psalmist chronicles
his struggle to meet his physical needs in light of the prosperity
of the wicked. As the psalmist works through feelings of jealousy
and envy, he admits in verse 3, "For I was envious of the arrogant; I
saw the prosperity of the wicked." Finding meaning in the seeming
disparity was impossible, so in frustration he gave up, and in verse
16 called it a "wearisome task." After a period of suffering, a visit
to the sanctuary of the Lord brought the needed transformation, as
he recounts in verses 23–26 (NRSV):

---

72. Westermann, *Praise and Lament*, 154.

73. Ellington rightly cautions readers of the Psalms against the "collapse of
the dialectic" that reduces lament to a mere "introduction to praise," and fails
to see its relationship to praise. Just as most of the laments eventually move
to praise, so too do many of the psalms of praise carry scars or memories of
suffering experienced at the other end of the continuum. For example, Pss 105
and 106, at first glance, are glorious celebrations of God's wondrous deliverance of his people from Egypt and their induction into the promised land.
However, within these psalms are shades of suffering, remembrance of sin,
rebellion, and judgment, the period of slavery in Egypt, feelings of hunger and
thirst, and fear at the crossing of the Red Sea. While the overall tone is praise, it
is clear that the suffering is what propelled the people towards celebration and
thanksgiving. Ellington, *Risking Truth*, 62.

23 Nevertheless I am continually
With you;
you hold my right hand.
24 you guide me with your counsel
and afterward you will receive
me with honor.
25 Whom have I in heaven but you?
And there is nothing on earth
that I desire other than you.
26 My flesh and my heart may fail,
but God is the strength of my
heart and my portion forever.

The psalmist's realignment and renewed identification with the faithful Torah community brings about the transformation. Brueggemann and Bellinger note the powerful "nevertheless" found in verse 23 that leads the psalmist back to the "elemental faith claim": Yahweh is good.[74] However, even the perception of Yahweh's goodness is transformed from "material prosperity" in verse 1, to a celebration of "intimate communion."[75]

Representing new orientation, Ps 30 is one of a group of psalms known as songs of thanksgiving.[76] Mays notes the importance of these psalms for the spiritual health of the community, and labels them a "canonical witness" whose expression completes the cycle of suffering in the psalmist's life, thus affecting the life of the community.[77] Though the suffering was experienced in isolation, deliverance from it is celebrated in community. Thus, the communal praise completes the cycle of suffering, becoming a natural and necessary element if the period of disorientation is to completely resolve into new orientation. Mays writes, "Its praise completes and consummates what was begun in supplication."[78]

74. Brueggemann and Bellinger, *Psalms*, 319.

75. Brueggemann and Bellinger, *Psalms*, 319.

76. Nowell, *Pleading Cursing, Praising*, 87. Included in the songs of thanksgiving are Pss 9; 10; 18; 30; 32; 34; 40:1–13; 41; 65; 66:13–20; 75; 107; 116; 118; 120; 124; 129; 138.

77. Mays, *Psalms*, 24.

78. Mays, *Psalms*, 140. Don E. Saliers notes that the call to rejoice in many psalms of thanksgiving was not "a call to conjure up objectless inner feelings

The transformation culminates in verses 11 and 12, which see the psalmist putting off his "sackcloth" only to be clothed with joy. Brueggemann and Bellinger draw attention to the "total reconfiguration" in the Hebrew verbs used here to mean "take off" and "put on," which indicate no less than complete transformation.[79] The use of such strong verbs can only indicate the depth of gratitude on the part of the psalmist for the miraculous salvation, transformation, and restoration to community which could come from Yahweh alone.

SPEECH-ACT THEORY APPLIED TO THE PSALMS OF LAMENT

Speech-act theory, developed by John Searle, Donald Evans, and others, was first presented systematically and in detail in the William James Lectures at Harvard University by J. L. Austin in 1955, and later in his book *How to Do Things with Words* in 1962.[80] Austin's foundational theories were further developed in seminal works by John Searle (1969 and 1979), and Herbert Paul Grice (2001), respectively.[81] As defined subsequently by Eugene Botha (2007), speech act theory is a theory of language that "focuses its attention on the effects of the use of certain utterances in a specific speech situation."[82] This theory was first applied early on to theological language by Donald Evans (1963) in *The Logic of*

---

of elation." The praise and thanksgiving was not a rush to rejoicing, but rather a *natural outgrowth* of the deliverance from suffering, and was freely offered, indeed *had to be offered*, if one was to fully enter into new orientation. Saliers, *Soul in Paraphrase*, 41.

79. Brueggemann and Bellinger, *Psalms*, 152. The authors note the correlation between these verbs and the baptismal formula of Eph 4:22–24 (NRSV), in which Paul admonishes the Ephesian church to "put away" the old self, and "clothe yourselves" with the new self, "created according to the likeness of God." This transformation is also one which evokes praise of the depth and intensity likely felt by the psalmist.

80. Botha, "Speech Act Theory," 275; Austin, *How to Do Things with Words*.

81. Grice, *Studies in the Way of Words*; Searle, *Speech Acts*; Searle, *Expression and Meaning*.

82. Botha, "Speech Act Theory," 276.

Self-Involvement: A Philosophical Study of Everyday Language with Special Reference to the Christian Use of Language about God as Creator, specifically drawing on Austin's theory of the performative nature of speech acts.[83] The development of the theory can be concisely introduced as follows.

Speech-act theorists Austin, Searle, and others, developed the concept of illocutionary and perlocutionary acts. An illocutionary act is defined as an act of "speaking or writing which in itself effects or constitutes the intended action, e.g., ordering, warning, or promising."[84] Perlocutionary acts represent "the consequences or *effects* such acts have on the actions, thoughts, or beliefs, etc., of hearers."[85] In *Expression and Meaning: Studies in the Theories of Speech Acts* (1979), Searle further delineated six categories of speech acts:

1. Assertives—describe/represent an existing state of affairs; a claim ("Save me, O God, by your name, and vindicate me by your might." Ps 54:1 (NRSV))

2. Directives—imperative command in an attempt to produce an action ("Be gracious to me, O LORD, for I am languishing." Ps 6:2 (NRSV))

3. Commissives—commit to a specific course of action in the future; vow, promise, swear ("I will sing to the LORD, because he has dealt bountifully with me." Ps 13:6 (NRSV))

4. Expressives—express a specific psychological state about a situation; thank, apologize, welcome, congratulate, etc. ("I will exult and rejoice in your steadfast love, because you have seen my affliction; you have taken heed of my adversities." Ps 31:7 (NRSV))

---

83. Evans, *Logic of Self-Involvement.*

84. "Illocutionary Act," Oxford Living Dictionary.

85. Searle, *Speech Acts*, 25, emphasis original. Johnson further delineates these two actions: an illocutionary act intends an action, though not completely clear on the exact outcome; a perlocutionary act is one which "produces an effect in its hearer/reader." Johnson, *Foundations for Soul Care*, 197.

5. Declarations—realization of a proposition ("Vindicate me, O LORD, my God, according to your righteousness, and do not let them rejoice over me." Ps 35:24 (NRSV))

6. Assertive declarative—an assertive with the force of a declaration ("The LORD is king! Let the earth rejoice; let the many coastlands be glad!" Ps 97:1 (NRSV))[86]

These six categories draw attention to the fact that speech is more than the actual words spoken, but is equally connected to the action or intention which is an outcome of what is said.[87] Searle also notes that more than one type of speech act can occur in the same statement.[88]

Donald Evans first applied speech-act theory to the biblical language of worship in *The Logic of Self-Involvement*.[89] Building on Austin's theories on speech acts, Evans argues that many statements found in Scripture can be labeled as "expressive" to some degree.[90] According to psalm scholar Gordon Wenham, Evans's assertion describes the prayers found in the Psalter, which were intended to be "recited or sung as prayers."[91] But Evans categorizes the psalms further. Due to their self-involving nature, the prayers of the Psalter according to Evans fall into two main speech-act categories: commissives (the speaker commits himself to a course of action: promise, pledge, engage, swear loyalty) and behabitives (an attitude is expressed: praise, thank, worship, protest).[92]

---

86. Searle, *Expression and Meaning*, 12–20.

87. Botha, "Speech Act Theory," 276.

88. Searle, *Expression and Meaning*, 50.

89. Evans, *Logic of Self-Involvement*.

90. Wenham, *Psalms as Torah*, 67.

91. Wenham, *Psalms as Torah*, 63, 67.

92. Wenham, *Psalms as Torah*, 67–68. Wenham notes that, here, Evans "does not use the more nuanced analysis of speech acts found in Searle's work; rather he builds on Austin's simpler understanding of performative acts. . . . He adopts the terminology of J. L. Austin . . . to define the character of worship language." Wenham, *Psalms as Torah*, 67.

Implications of Speech-Act Theory for Corporate Worship

Gordon Wenham argues that the application of speech-act theory to the Psalms sets them apart as performative speech unlike any other in Scripture. Wenham notes that Old Testament narratives or passages from the Law were likely recited within a family or tribe, and those listening could do so passively.[93] The use of the psalms, however, was a different act altogether, and required much more intentional action on the part of the worshiper. Instead of passive participation, the worshiper reciting the Psalms was likely to do so in a much more heartfelt and intentional manner. This is where consideration of the performative nature of the psalms comes into play for Wenham, especially in corporate use. Commissive and behabitive speech acts involve more than physical participation by the speaker or the one praying; they call for commitment and a lasting change of behavior at the heart level.

An interesting connection to speech-act theory is the concept of remembrance in the Old Testament, especially in the Psalms. Tim Keller notes that the concept of remembering, according to Scripture, is "controlling consciousness," or "making something so central to your consciousness that it affects you completely and particularly as a test of your behavior; to have it so central to your consciousness that it controls how you act."[94] Keller uses Ps 103 (NRSV) as an example of the psalmist "controlling [his own] consciousness" as he reminds himself of Yahweh's "benefits" in verses 3–5: "Who forgives all your iniquity, who heals all your diseases, who redeems your life from the Pit, who crowns you with steadfast love and mercy, who satisfies you with good as long as you live so that your youth is renewed like the eagle's." In verses 1 and 2, the psalmist speaks to himself in an "expressive" act, reminding himself in his inmost being not to simply *state* or *recite* these truths, but according to Keller, to engage them deeply through "vigorous disciplined meditation and contemplation."[95] The command to

93. Wenham, *Psalms as Torah*, 64.
94. Keller, "Praying the Gospel."
95. Keller, "Praying the Gospel."

"bless the LORD, O my soul" is therefore an expressive speech act because, by proclaiming Yahweh worthy to be blessed, the writer is offering to God awe and respect. The result of this awe and respect is a promise to meditate on Yahweh's goodness, to offer praise, and to remember his acts in a way that results in changed behavior.

The implications for speech-act theory in praying the lament psalms in corporate worship are many. First, to pray the psalms of lament corporately or individually in the sense discussed here can aid in the transformation of the suffering individual or group. Brueggemann notes the ability of these psalms to "evoke reality, thereby denying the tendency to the self-deception of a well-ordered life," or one which refuses to admit or process difficult emotions in God's presence, choosing instead to cover them with a façade of order and success.[96] The evoking of such reality is, according to Brueggemann, the very act that transforms faith, and which allows us to see God as "present in, participating in, and attentive to the . . . displacement of life."[97] It is in the bringing to speech of such sorrow that we can more readily identify with the Christ of Isa 53:3 (NRSV): "A man of suffering, and acquainted with infirmity." In addition to giving place and permission for such raw expressions, praying through the cycle of suffering found in the Psalms allows us to understand and expect the faithfulness of God to bring new orientation in the future.

Second, in addition to transformation, the bold language of the Psalms teaches us that nothing is out of bounds, and our pain, or the pain of others, must not be denied in our discourse with God.[98] This is especially noted in the imprecatory psalms, those which have been described by Wenham as "savage prayers" against those who do harm to God's people.[99] According to Wenham, these directive prayers have three important implications: (1) they help us identify with others who suffer, (2) the simple act of bringing to speech these concerns gives greater weight and focus to the

96. Brueggemann, *Message of the Psalms*, 53.

97. Brueggemann, *Message of the Psalms*, 52.

98. Brueggemann, *Message of the Psalms*, 52.

99. Wenham, *Psalms as Torah*, 167.

need, and (3) they can bring to light our own neglect in effecting change regarding violence in the world.[100]

Finally, the expressive nature of the psalms of lament reminds us of our mortality and finitude, and thereby renews our love for the message of the Gospel. The wide range of emotions and conditions covered by the lament psalms give language to myriad physical, mental, and spiritual states, including the sorrows which Christ bore on the cross. The psalms bring a multiplicity of expressions, including the cry for healing (Ps 6), repentance (Ps 51), deliverance from fear (Ps 3), expressing guilt and the need for forgiveness (Ps 130), and the struggle with doubt (Ps 73). Thus, their use in corporate worship can remind us that Christ not only died for our salvation, but also that we might experience abundant life paradoxically, even in the midst of our present suffering (John 10:10).

CONCLUSION

The dialogical nature of Israel's prayer life found in the Psalms gives evidence of a rich and fully alive relationship with God. Although a surface reading of the lament psalms can give the impression of a lack of trust in God's sovereignty, faithfulness, and steadfast love, a deeper look reveals a cry that appeals to the psalmist's knowledge of God's history of faithfulness to his people. The psalms of disorientation and new orientation give further evidence of this covenant relationship as the plea and complaint are transformed. It is then that the psalmist offers praise to God who has not only restored the sufferer but has repaired the breach in community so vital to the worship life of Israel. So, while many of the laments present themselves as individual, the heart of the psalmist's brokenness is ultimately communal, thus his call for rejoicing amongst the community at the time of his or her deliverance.

100. Wenham, *Psalms as Torah*, 177–78. McCann notes that the use of imprecation in prayer puts vengeance into the hands of God, where it rightfully belongs. Additionally, in praying these psalms, believers are reminded of previous deliverance, or the deliverance of others, from similar circumstances. McCann, *Theological Introduction to the Psalms*, 117–19.

The cry of the sufferer, however, does not cease at the coming of Christ. Indeed, Christ consistently modeled in his own prayers the use of the lament psalms in processing his own suffering. The following chapter explores the continuance of lament in Christ's prayers found in the Gospels. Chapter 4 continues with an exploration of the ways in which key New Testament Epistle writers such as Paul, Peter, and John followed Christ's example and drew from the rich treasure of the Psalms in articulating their personal suffering and the suffering of the persecuted first-century church. These themes and key scriptural passages are explored in the next chapters to demonstrate the continued historical trajectory of the use of lament psalms, both individually and corporately in the lives of believers.

3

Models of Lament in the Life of Jesus

The other gods were strong; but Thou wast weak;
They rode, but Thou didst stumble to a throne;
But to our wounds Only God's wounds speak;
And not a god has wounds, but Thou alone.[1]

—EDWARD SHILLITO

THE MOST IMPORTANT MODEL for the use of Old Testament prayers of lament in the New Testament is Jesus Christ. During his earthly life, as recorded by the Gospel writers, Christ voiced his suffering and modeled for believers the use of prayers of lament from the Old Testament in processing his experiences and emotions. The Gospels recount three important scenes in which Christ lamented: (1) his lament over Jerusalem due to unrepentant sin

1. Edward Shillito, "Jesus of the Scars," as cited in Carson, *How Long, O Lord?*, 191.

(Matt 23:37–39; Luke 13:34–35); (2) the death of Lazarus (John 11:34–44); and (3) the cry of dereliction from the cross (Ps 22:1). Although not directly quoting the Psalms, Jesus' grief over his own impending death, expressed in prayer to the Father in the garden of Gethsemane, references laments found in the Psalms.

JESUS LAMENTS OVER JERUSALEM

Prior to his lament over the city of Jerusalem over unrepentant sin (Matt 23:37–39; Luke 13:34–35), Jesus upbraids the scribes and Pharisees for their hypocritical, pompous behavior (Matt 23:1–7) and ill treatment of their fellow Jews. Jesus was clearly displeased by their self-indulgence that resulted in increased pain and suffering for the people for whom they were supposed to care. Labeling them "blind guides" (Matt 23:16 NRSV), "whitewashed tombs" (Matt 23:27 NRSV), "snakes," and "brood of vipers" (Matt 23: 33 NRSV), Jesus uses strong language in calling attention to their sinful behaviors that had persisted despite repeated calls for repentance from the prophets (Matt 23:34a) whom they had killed, crucified, flogged, and persecuted (Matt 23:34b). Prior to Jesus' diatribe in Matthew 23, the Jewish leaders in Jerusalem had demonstrated a history of misrule in alliance with Roman political leaders, all for selfish gain and accumulation of power.[2]

Jesus' rebuke of the religious leaders of Jerusalem was not only due to their mistreatment of the Jewish population, but also in the context of his exposing the corruption in this city which had been celebrated for centuries in the Psalms as God's "holy habitation" (Ps 46:4 NRSV), and the "city of our God" (Pss 48:1, 87:3 NRSV). Tragically, instead of being celebrated and revered as such, the city and God's house had become a den of thieves, desecrated by the greed and corruption of the Jewish priesthood, and the city itself was under the occupation and rule of polytheistic Rome. Jesus knew God's pattern of divine judgment of Israel's sin in the past and God's decision to send his people into exile as punishment for their

---

2. Carter, "Matthew 23:37–39," 66.

sins. The people's repeated rejection of God continued, even though Jesus had come to bring the good news of God's love, salvation, and new covenant to the people. Thus, one finds in Matt 23:37–39 and Luke 13:34–35 this record of Jesus' lament over the sins of the people, their rejection of him as the Messiah, and the tragedy that Jerusalem, which was God's holy city, had fallen so low.[3]

Following his angry rebuke, Jesus pours out his grief in a kind of city lament that strongly echoes Jeremiah's famous use of the genre in Lamentations. However, this lament of Jesus is not only over Jerusalem but by implication the sins of the nation of Israel and the whole world. Tremper Longman III identifies this famous lament imagery drawn directly from the Psalms, when Jesus lovingly expresses his longing to "gather" the people together "as a hen gathers her brood under her wings" (Matt 23:37; Luke 13:34 NRSV).[4] With almost maternal-like instinct, Jesus uses the metaphor found in the Psalms of a mother hen protecting her young from potential threats. The psalmists, according to Longman, repeatedly used this metaphor (17:8, 36:7, 57:1, 61:4, 63:7, 91:4) to "suggest the image of a bird shielding its young with its wings, or perhaps driving potential threats away from its young with the rapid beating of its wings."[5] This expression of Christ's love and compassion for the people is remarkable given the extent of their sins, their killing of the prophets, their repeated violation of their covenant with Yahweh, and their rejection of Jesus as the Messiah.

Following the metaphor of the hen gathering her brood, Jesus revealed the result of the peoples' rejection in Matt 23:37 NRSV

3. Carter, "Matthew 23:37–39," 67.

4. Longman, *Psalms*, 233.

5. Longman, *Psalms*, 233. The image of the mother bird would likely have been familiar to the people of Israel. Moses used the illustration in Deut 32:11 in his final song before his death. In v. 11, Moses used the image of an eagle that "stirs up its nest, that flutters over its young, spreading out its wings, catching them, bearing them on its pinions." God had guided the people out of Egypt and into the promised land with utmost and constant provision. Jesus could have been evoking this imagery and memory of Moses' song to remind the people, not only of God's care, but also of his covenant which they had repeatedly violated. Longman, *Psalms*, 233.

(Luke 13:35 NRSV): "See, your house is left to you, desolate." This judgment was likely leveled at both the city of Jerusalem and the temple, both of which were the representational seat of God's rule and reign.[6] That God would leave the city and temple "desolate" was significant, given its central place in Israel's history and in God's purpose. When Jesus rode into Jerusalem on a donkey in Matthew 21:1–11, he was fulfilling the prophecy found in Zech 9:9 of the coming King of Zion who would rule in righteousness, bringing salvation. This judgment on the current religious leaders of Jerusalem and its inhabitants was the result of their repeated sin and rejection of God as their sovereign king.[7]

According to Warren Carter, the lament of Jesus over Jerusalem mirrors the "three-part . . . pattern in which Israel sins, God punishes (exiles) [her], and restores Israel."[8] This pattern is found in the Old Testament in the words of the prophets each time Israel breaks its covenant with Yahweh. However, judgment for the sins of the people is not final, as God wondrously promises eventual restoration even as the people are being exiled.[9] This pattern of sin, judgment, and restoration seems to be evoked in Jesus' lament when he declares, "For I tell you, you will not see me again, until you say, 'Blessed is the one who comes in the name of the Lord'"

---

6. Carter, "Matthew 23:27–39," 67.

7. Both Luke and Matthew record the triumphal entry of Jesus into Jerusalem riding on a donkey (Matt 21:1–11; Luke 19:28–40). However, only Luke follows this with the record of Jesus again weeping over Jerusalem following his entry on the donkey (Luke 19:41–44). Here again, Jesus foretells the coming destruction of the city in AD 70. He wept, stating, "If you, even you, had recognized on this day the things that make for peace! But now they are hidden from your eyes. . . . And they will not leave within you one stone upon another in you, because you did not recognize the time of your visitation from God." (vv. 42, 44b NRSV)

8. Carter, "Matthew 23:27–39," 68.

9. Pss 105 and 106 chronicle the history of Israel, including their sins and violation of Yahweh's covenant, along with the promised restoration. Brueggemann and Bellinger note the use of "three verbs" in Ps 106:6 to describe the extent of the people's sin: "sinned," "committed iniquity," and "done wickedness." The repetition gives weight to and emphasizes the egregious nature of their wrongdoing. Brueggemann and Bellinger, *Psalms*, 459.

(Matt 23:39 NRSV). Mirroring Yahweh's promise of restoration, Jesus seems to draw from Ps 118:26 (NRSV), in promising restoration of the people after they are once again judged for their sin.[10] At some point in their future, the people would turn to Christ, recognizing him as their Messiah, and declare, "Blessed is the one who comes in the name of the LORD!"

JESUS LAMENTS THE DEATH OF LAZARUS

Jesus' lament over the death of Lazarus is the only recorded example of Jesus expressing his personal grief over the loss of a friend. Scripture records that Jesus loved Martha, Mary, and Lazarus, and seems to imply a deeply personal and meaningful relationship with this family. According to John 11:33 (NRSV), a few days after Lazarus's death, upon meeting Mary and the other Jews who had come to weep with her, he was "greatly disturbed in spirit and deeply moved." In his record of this event in Jesus' life, John succinctly records perhaps the single most poignant verse in all of Scripture: "Jesus began to weep" (John 11:35 NRSV). Seeing Lazarus's tomb and hearing the weeping of family and friends moved Jesus to a tearful expression of grief and sadness.

The reference to Psalms in this lament by Jesus is indirect, but some connections can be drawn. In describing Jesus' response to the death of his friend, John seems to draw from Psalms, stating that he was "deeply moved" (John 11:33 NRSV), and "greatly disturbed" (John 11: 38 NRSV). The phrases "deeply moved" and "greatly disturbed" are used throughout the Psalms to describe grief, or suffering brought on by sickness, suffering, or the enemy. It would seem that John drew most clearly from Ps 6:3 (NRSV): "My soul is struck with terror, while you, O LORD–how long?" Again, in Ps 77:4b (NRSV), the psalmist states, "I am so troubled

10. Brueggemann and Bellinger, *Psalms*, 506. According to Longman, this psalm, an entrance liturgy, is the final psalm in the Egyptian Hallel, which was sung during Passover in the peoples' celebration of the exodus from Egypt. Whether this psalm refers specifically to the exodus from Egypt or another deliverance from battle is unclear. Longman, *Psalms*, 399.

that I cannot speak." Echoing the Psalms, this language is used to describe a time of sorrow and suffering in the life of Jesus, and clearly connects to the prophecy that he was "a man of suffering, and acquainted with infirmity" (Isa 53:3 NRSV).[11]

JESUS' PRAYER IN THE GARDEN OF GETHSEMANE

Three of the four Gospel writers (Matthew, Mark, and Luke) give a full account of Jesus' prayer in the garden of Gethsemane prior to his arrest and crucifixion.[12] This prayer, in which Jesus prays to the Father to remove "the cup" from him is an expression of not only Jesus' lament, but also an expression of fear and anguish.[13] However, whether or not the emotion of fear is present, that Jesus would be "sorrowful" and "greatly troubled" indicates a deep level of distress. That Jesus was experiencing some intense distress is

11. Rebekah Eklund notes that the death and raising of Lazarus (John 11:40) functions similarly as the death and resurrection of Jesus (John 21:19) in that both would bring glory to God. Eklund writes, "The parallels between the deaths of Lazarus and Jesus provide an ironic sting to this scene and to Jesus' weeping: it is the raising of Lazarus that precipitates Jesus' arrest and crucifixion in John's narrative (John 11:45-53, 12:9-11); but it is also Jesus' confrontation with death at Lazarus's tomb that prefigures God's victory over death at Jesus' resurrection." Eklund, *Jesus Wept*, 38-39.

12. John places Jesus and the disciples in an unnamed garden just prior to his arrest and crucifixion. There is, however, no record of his prayer as recorded in Matt 26:36-46 or Mark 14:32-42.

13. Gerald Peterman also describes Jesus' emotional reaction in Matt 26:37 NRSV ("grieved and agitated") and Mark 14:33-34 NRSV ("greatly distressed and agitated") as one of fear, in addition to agitation. Peterman notes that this is the first time Jesus experienced the wrath of the Father, and the emotive response is evidence of one completely unfamiliar with this, given he had always pleased the Father (John 8:29). Peterman notes, "And yet the certainty of his obedient death does not take away the temptation to go the easy way; nor does his certainty make him a stoic as he faces wrath." Gerald W. Peterman, "A Man of Sorrows: Emotions and the Suffering of Jesus," in Peterman and Schmutzer, *Between Pain and Grace*, 83-102. Scott Bader-Saye emphasizes the use of the Greek word translated as "frightened" or "greatly amazed," in the previous references. He notes that this is the only time this term is used in conjunction with Jesus throughout the Gospels. Scott Bader-Saye, "Fear in the Garden," 10.

supported by the description of his posture: "He threw himself on the ground" (Matt 26:39 and Mark 14:35 NRSV). Only in Luke's account (22:41 NRSV) does one read that Jesus simply "knelt down" to pray.[14]

These descriptions of Jesus' demeanor and posture during prayer would seem to find some connections in the lament psalms, which use similar language. Since Jesus used the language of the lament psalms elsewhere, he could have possibly had in mind Ps 6:3 (NRSV), which specifically states, "My soul is also struck with terror." This psalm, along with Ps 42, is known as the psalm of the "righteous sufferer," due to the opening inscription in Greek manuscripts translated "unto the end."[15] Eklund notes, "The Gospels display a common pattern of Jesus using the lament psalms to express his struggle over the coming time of eschatological trial as well as his trust in God and his desire to accomplish God's will."[16]

In addition to his possible appropriation of language found in Ps 6, Jesus seems to borrow another common metaphor from the Psalms: the cup. This metaphor is used in the Psalms to indicate either God's favor or his wrath. Ps 16:5 (NRSV) finds the writer declaring, "The Lord is my chosen portion and my cup; you hold my lot." Ps 23:5b (NRSV) presents a theme of abundant provision from the Lord, his shepherd, stating, "My cup overflows." Alternatively, the metaphor of the cup can also refer to God's wrath poured out on those who sin or who break his covenant.[17] Ps 75:8 (NRSV) states, "For in the hand of the LORD there is a cup, with foaming wine, well mixed; he will pour a draught from it, and all the wicked

14. Eklund points to the influence of Stoic philosophy and Luke's Greco-Roman social environment that demonstrated an aversion to public displays of sorrow. The influence of Stoicism and Greco-Roman social structure are, according to Eklund, a possible explanation for his choice of "knelt down," which is a more composed response. Eklund, *Jesus Wept*, 30.

15. Eklund, *Jesus Wept*, 38. Eklund notes the eschatological function of these lament psalms in Qumran literature which made it much more likely that the Gospel writers interpreted them this way as well.

16. Eklund, *Jesus Wept*, 38.

17. Futato, Mark D. "Psalms 16 and 23: Confidence in a Cup," in Schmutzer and Howard, *Psalms*, 231–36.

of the earth shall drain it down to the dregs." Ps 11:6 (NRSV) cites the ingredients of the cup of wrath as "a scorching wind." While Ps 102:9 (NRSV) does not directly reference "the cup," it indicates that the psalmist's drink is mingled with his own tears, which would imply emotions connected to lament. That Jesus would pray for the removal of "the cup" (Matt 26:39, 42; Mark 14:36, 39; Luke 22:42 NRSV) indicates therefore that he understood and was familiar with the psalmic metaphors and suggests strongly that he likely borrowed from them as he wrestled with the coming weight and severity of God's wrath he would have to bear.

Not only does one find connection to Jesus' use of these psalmic metaphors, but also to the overall purpose in the laments of bringing to speech one's suffering, demonstrated in Jesus' appeal to the Father: "If it is possible, let this cup pass from me" (Matt 26:39 NRSV). This practice of bringing to speech one's suffering is consistently found in Brueggemann's cycle of "orientation, dis-orientation, and reorientation" in the Psalms, which itself could possibly even be applied in this broader sense to Jesus' prayer in Gethsemane, his crucifixion, and resurrection. His knowledge of the coming "cup" of God's wrath, the severe beating he would endure, the brutality and inhumane nature of the crucifixion that Jesus had likely witnessed others endure, and his betrayal by Judas produced unmitigated dread and suffering, resulting in a depth of disorientation not previously known by any other human. Yet, in his resurrection, a degree of new orientation not previously known also occurred and could be connected to the statement in Hebrews 12:2 (NRSV): "Looking to Jesus, the pioneer and perfecter of our faith, who for the sake of the joy that was set before him endured the cross [disorientation], disregarding its shame, and has taken his seat at the right hand of the throne of God [new orientation]."

JESUS' CRY OF DERELICTION FROM THE CROSS

Although Jesus modeled the use of biblical lament throughout his life, nowhere is it clearer than in his cry of dereliction from the cross recorded in Matt 27:46 (NRSV): "My God, my God, why have you forsaken me?" In quoting Ps 22 to express the abandonment he experienced in the crucifixion, Jesus is continuing the Old Testament liturgical tradition of using the lament psalms to express sorrow to God, and also giving permission to all who live after him to use these psalms in the same way.[18] James Mays notes that in this psalm one does not hear the voice of a particular sufferer at a certain point in history; instead, "its language was designed to give individuals a poetic and liturgical location, to provide a prayer that is paradigmatic for particular suffering and needs. To use it was to set oneself in its paradigm."[19] Jesus shows all people who would come after him how to suffer righteously by joining together with those who trusted Yahweh before him and praying in their words.

As believers today read Jesus' use of Ps 22:1 in the gospel accounts, their experience of suffering can be transformed through the power of Christ's innocent and redemptive suffering. Mays notes that often during a time of suffering, "faith and experience" come into conflict with one another, as they did most acutely in Christ's crucifixion.[20] Mays comments:

> In [Psalm 22] dying is portrayed as the experience of a threefold loss: of vitality, of social support, and of God. It was clear that where death set the final seal on that threefold experience for those who identified themselves with the Lord, a line was drawn against God's sovereignty.... In the passion of Jesus, that threefold loss is undergone and he dies. But his resurrection is the signal to all who dread and undergo the threefold loss that death itself has been brought within the rule of the God of Jesus Messiah.[21]

---

18. The early church recognized Jesus as the fulfillment of the Psalms. Ps 22, although not a royal psalm (such as Pss 2 and 72) that celebrates the anointing of a king, was nonetheless associated with Christ. This association was due in part because the psalm expressed humiliation and eventual vindication of Christ. Similar psalms include 31, 69, and 118. Galvin, "Messianic Psalms," 335–36.

19. Mays, "Prayer and Christology," 323.

20. Mays, "Prayer and Christology," 330.

21. Mays, "Prayer and Christology," 330–31.

In Christ's resurrection, the conflict between "faith and experience" is ultimately resolved and is "a justification of God in whom they trust, and a vindication of their trust."[22] Jesus' crucifixion and resurrection assure believers that God has not failed, nor have they been forgotten.

Throughout the New Testament, the believer's participation in the suffering of Christ is a consistent theme. The appeal for help found in the Psalms has shifted to an acceptance of suffering "for the sake of Christ," which submits our pain to God's glory and his overarching plan.[23] With this shift comes the impact of the cross, which does not negate suffering or take away our right to lament. Instead, the cross ensures us that our suffering is not in vain, and that it will ultimately be redemptive. This tension is noted in Paul's writings (Rom 8:28; 2 Cor 4:17), Peter's first epistle (1 Pet 1:6–7) and James' admonition to rejoice in the midst of fiery trials (Jas 1:2–4).

Ellington claims, "Suffering and the function of lament are changed in light of the death and resurrection of Christ."[24] The reason for the changed function of suffering is the added element of the "already-but-not-yet" in the life of believers as a result of Christ's death and resurrection. In his study of eschatological themes in modern worship song, Matthew Westerholm notes, "Following Christ's ascension, the church lives in the days when the Bridegroom has been taken away from them (Matt 9:15). This is a season to lament."[25] While on the one hand God's "power is made perfect in weakness," we still experiences times of suffering during which the cry of lament is necessary. Ellington writes, "Instead of seeking for a hidden God in the midst of suffering, the New Testament lament accompanies, and even impels, the coming of God's response to suffering, the ministry of Messiah."[26] The cries of New Testament believers demonstrate that Christ's prayer, "Thy

---

22. Mays, "Prayer and Christology," 330–31.

23. Miller, *They Cried to the Lord*, 323.

24. Ellington, *Risking Truth*, 171.

25. Westerholm, "'Hour Is Coming and Is Now Here,'" 190.

26. Ellington, *Risking Truth*, 180.

kingdom come," has yet to be fulfilled. While the momentary in-breaking of his kingdom is felt in acts of healing, provision, and deliverance, those cries that await to be heard remind us that his kingdom is yet to come.

CHRISTOLOGICAL IMPLICATIONS FOR A NEW TESTAMENT THEOLOGY OF LAMENT AND SUFFERING IN THE EPISTLES

The life, crucifixion, and resurrection of Christ form much of the foundation upon which the New Testament theology of suffering is built, as previously noted.[27] Themes of the redemptive nature of Christ's work pervade the New Testament, even infusing and weaving together Old Testament themes of hope in the coming of a victorious messiah with the reality of the suffering servant and his subsequent identification with the suffering of his people. The honest, heartfelt dialogue in the Gospels between Jesus and those in need continued to echo the Old Testament communal cries of disorientation. Jesus' use of Old Testament laments in shaping his prayers connected believers to Israel even as they fulfilled the nation's longing for messiah.[28] The question and subsequent answer to the purpose of suffering, which the Old Testament viewed largely as a consequence of sin, was redefined and became "a thesis, if not *the* thesis," of the New Testament, according to Dan G.

27. Ellington, *Risking Truth*, 168.
28. Eklund, *Jesus Wept*, 171.

McCartney.[29] He notes, "The answer to the problem of suffering and death lies in the suffering and death of Jesus Christ."[30]

Christ's incarnational suffering and work of redemption on the cross shifted and redefined the purpose of suffering for believers. In fact, Christ's redemptive work is multifaceted, not only saving sinners from eternal judgment, guilt, and brokenness, but also continuing this salvific work as he identifies with us in our present suffering. In writing on the diversity of these atonement images found in the cross, Richard Mouw observes:

> The fact is that the Bible presents the work of the Cross as a many-faceted event, setting forth a variety of images for the Atonement: self-giving love, the forgiveness of enemies, payment of a debt, the ransom of captives, victory over the demonic principalities and powers, and so on.[31]

This wide spectrum of images depicts Christ as victorious and powerful, while also revealing him as the broken Christ of Isa 53:3 (NRSV) who was a "man of suffering, and acquainted with infirmity." This paradox is echoed throughout the New Testament.

The two great extremes in this multiplicity of images of Jesus are those of *Christus Victor*, an "unbroken Christ, a powerful, conquering Christ," and *Christus dolor*, "one who suffered and is sorrowful."[32] While the doctrine of atonement in Scripture is vast, the images of the victorious Christ and the suffering Christ are central and focus on different and vital views of Christ's life, as well

---

29. Dan McCartney, "Suffering and the Goodness of God in the Gospels," in Morgan and Peterson, *Suffering and the Goodness*, 79–94, emphasis original. McCartney notes that the Old Testament dealt with the suffering of the innocent through a theology of "vicarious suffering of the righteous remnant of Israel as a whole," as noted in Isa 53, and by enduring suffering, this remnant would "vicariously atone for the sins of Israel. This representative suffering would then qualify Israel as a whole for redemption." McCartney, "Suffering and the Goodness of God in the Gospels," in Morgan and Peterson, *Suffering and the Goodness*, 80.

30. McCartney, Dan. "Suffering and the Goodness of God in the Gospels," in Morgan and Peterson, *Suffering and the Goodness*, 80–94.

31. Mouw, "Why Christus Victor Is Not Enough," 30.

32. Mouw and Sweeney, *Suffering and Victorious Christ*, 3, 10.

as his redemptive work on the cross. While an in-depth examination of atonement is clearly not the focus here, the implications of both the victorious and suffering Christ to a New Testament understanding of lament practices are vital to the present study. Within Christ's suffering and death, one finds the paradoxical appearance of these two images. Viewed in juxtaposition, the images of the suffering and victorious Christ continue to model the cycle of disorientation (suffering) and new orientation (victorious) found in the Psalms and continuing in the lives of believers.

Christus Victor: The Conquering Christ

The image of *Christus victor*, or the conquering Christ, is found in Cols 2:13–15 (NRSV), as described by Paul:

> And when you were dead in trespasses and the uncircumcision of your flesh, God made you alive together with him, when he forgave us all our trespasses, erasing the record that stood against us with its legal demands. He set this aside, nailing it to the cross. He disarmed the rulers and authorities and made a public example of them, triumphing over them in it.[33]

The image of the victorious Christ is one of authority, of a Christ who conquers, defeating his enemies openly for all to see. This image of Christ was first embraced by church fathers including Origen, Irenaeus, and Gregory of Nyssa, and was often accepted as the "standard view" of early Christians with regard to atonement.[34]

---

33. The King James Version of this texts translates the final phrase of v. 15 as "triumphing over them by his cross."

34. Erickson, *Christian Theology*, 793. Schmiechen offers an exploration of ten theories of atonement, including that of liberation, which was connected to the image of Christ as victor in the early centuries of the Christian church. Schmiechen gives particular attention to the views of Iraneaus, Gregory of Nyssa, Athanasius, Jürgen Moltmann, James Cone, Gustavo Gutiérrez, and feminist and womanist perspectives with regard to the development of the liberation theory of atonement and its implications for modern views of Christ as victor. Schmiechen, *Saving Power*, 123–66.

In more recent years, the vision of Christ victorious in his atoning work has been strongly developed by Gustav Aulén in his book *Christus Victor: An Historical Study of the Three Main Types of the Atonement.* Aulén's book presents Christ as the beloved Son whom God sends into the battle against Satan in order to free all of humankind from certain defeat and eternal slavery.[35] While Jesus may have appeared to be defeated due to his suffering and horrific death at the hand of Satan, he ultimately defeated the enemy and rose again, promising a future restoration during which all humankind will rule with him in his kingdom.[36] Therefore, the cross is, in Mouw's words, not only a display of "more loving humanness," but also a picture of the battle between God and evil.[37] Instead of responding in violence and destruction, Christ defeated the political and military powers of Roman authorities who represented evil spiritual principalities by his nonviolent response, culminating in the ultimate victory of his resurrection.[38]

Since the publication of Aulén's book, other authors have embraced this view, including Gregory Boyd in *God at War: The Bible and Spiritual Conflict* and Robert Webber in *Ancient-Future Faith: Rethinking Evangelicalism for a Post-Modern World.*[39] More recently, Martyn John Smith, in *Divine Violence and the Christus Victor Atonement Model: God's Reluctant Use of Violence for Soteriological Ends*, posits that the *Christus victor* model presents a holistic view of God and salvation history. Smith notes:

> The CVM [*Christus victor* model] therefore does more than merely provide understanding and insight into the atonement; like one of its descriptors, the Dramatic Model, it presents the atonement of Christ as more than something which occurred only in the last week of his life on earth. Instead the CVM is an atonement model which focuses on God—what he set up, what he won

---

35. Aulén, *Christus Victor*, 16–17.
36. Harper, "Christus Victor, Postmodernism," 37.
37. Mouw, "Why Christus Victor Is Not Enough," 30.
38. Mouw, "Why Christus Victor Is Not Enough," 30.
39. Boyd, *God at War*; and Webber, *Ancient-Future Faith.*

back, and how his purposes are always fulfilled regardless of what Satan or humanity does to oppose him.[40]

In his examination of multiple atonement views, theologian
Paul Fiddes notes that the renaissance of the *Christus victor* atonement model since the publication of Aulén's book in 1931, is not
surprising given the increased attention in recent decades to issues
such as oppression and violence which necessitate a "divine victory over the hostile powers."[41]

Christus Dolor: The Suffering Christ

The image of *Christus dolor,* or the suffering Christ, presents the
"man of suffering, and acquainted with infirmity" (Isa 53:3 NRSV)
who, in his earthly life, suffered in solidarity with humankind.[42]
Drawing from this suffering servant passage in Isa 53, the image
of *Christus dolor* connects immediately with the image of a Christ
who identifies with us in our sufferings, as stated by the writer in
Heb 4:15 (NRSV): "For we do not have a high priest who is unable to sympathize with our weaknesses, but we have one who in
every respect has been tested as we are, yet without sin." According
to Mouw and Sweeney, the "identifying-with aspect" of Christ's
incarnation must be equally considered alongside his triumphant
resurrection, "the final redemptive transaction at Calvary."[43] As
the authors assert, the fact that God would so interest himself in
understanding humanity's brokenness "from the inside of our humanness" deserves to be taught and fully understood in all of its
implications for Christian living.[44]

The implications of *Christus dolor* for Christian living have
been embraced by both Western and non-Western theologians.
Theologians such as Kazoh Kitamori see Christ's ongoing work of

40. Smith, *Divine Violence,* 194.

41. Fiddes, *Past Event and Present Salvation,* 112.

42. Mouw and Sweeney, *Suffering and Victorious Christ,* 45–46.

43. Mouw and Sweeney, *Suffering and Victorious Christ,* 48.

44. Mouw and John Sweeney, *Suffering and Victorious Christ,* 48.

reconciliation and healing not only in his crucifixion, but in his identification with suffering throughout his earthly life.[45] Mouw and Sweeney point out the almost exclusive identification with Christ's suffering among non-Western theologians in works such as Kazoh Kitamori's *Theology of the Pain of God* and Kosuke Koyama's *Mount Fuji and Mount Sinai: A Critique of Idols*.[46] Western theologians such as Stephen J. Nichols and Jonathan Ebel argue that connections between war and religion in American society encourage support of the *Christus victor* model, and as Ebel notes, deflects the church away from identifying with the suffering Christ.[47]

CONCLUSION

As has been discussed in this chapter, both atonement theories of the victorious and suffering Christ respectively, are profoundly and carefully rooted in Scripture. Instead of embracing one model and rejecting the other, it can be argued that both are not only applicable but essential to a full grasp of the redemptive work of Christ. While Christ's life provides the ultimate examples of human suffering, in his identification with humankind culminating in the horrific agonies of his crucifixion, his triumph over death provides the basis of hope that the same resurrection life will ultimately be shared by all believers. Precisely by embracing these two opposing Christological images of the spectrum of suffering, we can more readily understand Paul's admonition in Rom 12:15, (NRSV) to "rejoice with those who rejoice, [and] weep with those who weep." The community of faith should expect to give and receive no less in its pursuit of Christocentric transformational living.

45. Kitamori, *Theology of the Pain of God*.

46. Kitamori, *Theology of the Pain of God*; Koyama, *Mount Fuji and Mount Sinai*.

47. Nichols, *Jesus Made in America*, 18; Ebel, *Faith in the Fight*, 112.

4

Suffering and Lament in the New Testament

THE INDIVIDUAL AND CORPORATE prayer life of Israel is most clearly articulated in the book of Psalms. The dialogical nature of the book reveals a number of themes, including the cry of the sufferer in the laments. As noted in the previous chapter, biblical expressions of lament, both individual and corporate, were rooted in the covenantal relationship between God and his people. When lived experience did not line up with God's covenant promises, the people cried out, and these cries of complaint and protest were recorded as part of the worship life of Israel.

Jesus' use of the psalms of lament in his own prayers during times of suffering, and particularly the Psalms, is reflected in the Gospels, in the lives of the New Testament writers and in the worship of first-century believers.[1] As noted in the previous chapter, not only did Jesus model *how* to lament through using the Psalms, but in serving as an example, he also gave believers *permission* to offer honest prayers of lament when experiencing suffering and

1. Moyise and Menken, *Psalms in the New Testament*, 1.

distress. Jesus demonstrated the need for bringing the emotions of suffering to speech, and that believers should pray these emotions in pre-reflective outpouring to God.[2] Thus, one can conclude that the dialogical nature of Israel's relationship with God demonstrated in the psalms and throughout the Old Testament did not end at the coming of Christ.

Jesus' use of the Psalms is obviously unparalleled, and is in itself sufficient to make the case for their continued use in corporate worship. The fact that the Psalms, along with Isaiah, are the Old Testament books most referenced, quoted, and alluded to by the New Testament writers further emphasizes the need for their inclusion in our individual and corporate worship today.[3] Their rich, artistic, and pictorial language should serve, in the words of Tremper Longman, as a "libretto of the most vibrant worship imaginable."[4]

Jesus and the New Testament writers use a broad range of the Psalms didactically, as well as in personal and corporate worship. This chapter contains a survey of lament psalms found in the New Testament, using Rebekah Eklund's typology of psalmic "echoes," "extensions," and "allusions."[5] Given the pervasiveness of the psalms in the New Testament, a study is merited of the specific use of lament psalms in the synoptic Gospels, letters, and epistles, whether in direct quotation or allusion. These echoes and extensions informed the New Testament writers' theology of suffering and served as the lens through which they understood and applied the implications of Jesus' suffering and resurrection to the ongoing suffering of believers.[6] This chapter addresses the New Testament writers' emphasis on the communal nature of suffering, and the subsequent implications of insights and themes from the laments for current evangelical corporate worship practices.

---

2. Keller, "Praying Your Tears."

3. Moyise and Menken, *Psalms in the New Testament*, 2.

4. Longman, *Psalms*, 9.

5. Eklund, *Jesus Wept*, 170.

6. Eklund, *Jesus Wept*, 170.

"ECHOES AND EXTENSIONS" OF OLD TESTAMENT LAMENT IN THE NEW TESTAMENT

The New Testament finds similarities to the Old Testament regarding practices of prayer.[7] Patrick Miller notes certain key similarities, for example, between the prayers of the Old Testament and those of both Paul and Jesus.[8] Miller observes that Jesus was "nurtured in the traditions of Israelite and Jewish prayer," and therefore it is not surprising to find metaphors from the Psalms and other Old Testament passages woven into his prayers, as discussed in the preceding chapter.[9] More importantly, Jesus demonstrated the breadth and depth of relationship with Yahweh and the broad emotional spectrum found in the Psalms when he prayed from the cross the desperate, anguished prayer, "My God, my God, why have you forsaken me?" (Ps 22:1 NRSV), followed by the contrasting and trust-filled expression, "Into your hands I commit my spirit" (Ps 31:5a NRSV). Paul mirrored the psalmists in his prayers for mercy, peace, and well-being, both for himself and first century believers.[10]

Eklund notes that, while the Psalms were used in quotes or allusions, the way in which the lament was shaped by the New Testament writers differed from that expressed in ancient Israel.[11] This difference in shape was due in part to the infusion of Stoic philosophy into the New Testament Epistles and the early church, and its emphasis on piety, and the emerging theology of the cross, which calls for "imitation of Christ's sacrificial self-giving" as noted

7. Eklund, *Jesus Wept*, 170. This section will implement Eklund's typology of "echoes and extensions" lament psalms found in the New Testament.

8. Miller, *They Cried to the Lord*, 305.

9. Miller, *They Cried to the Lord*, 305.

10. Miller, *They Cried to the Lord*, 305. It is important to note the corporate nature of Paul's prayers, which should serve as a model for believers today. Ephesians 3:14–21 records Paul's prayer for emotional and spiritual strength for Ephesian believers; Phil 1:9–11 contains Paul's prayer for loving relationship that connected to the spiritual help of believers; finally, Col 1:9–12 finds Paul praying holistically for believers for mental, spiritual, emotional, and even physical growth and maturity. These prayers mirror the psalmists who regularly wove these themes into their dialogue with Yahweh.

11. Eklund, *Jesus Wept*, 12.

in Phil 2:1–11.[12] While the lament as protest is present, Eklund
notes that the New Testament writers often emphasized lament as
penitence, which partially turns away from lament as protest, as in
Paul's use of Ps 51 in Rom 3.[13]

While themes of piety, joyful endurance, and penitence are
indeed present in the writings of Paul and others, references to
lament in the face of persecution can also be found. Eklund notes
the presence of an eschatological thrust in New Testament lament
that "trusts that God acts in the present through Jesus' resurrection and the sending of the Holy Spirit, and that God will act in
the future through the ultimate redemption and restoration of all
creation."[14] While Jesus' suffering changed the face and purpose
of lament, it did not effectively remove suffering which leads to
lament. Eklund notes:

> Jesus' proclamation of the kingdom and his death and
> resurrection signify the proleptic end of lament: Jesus
> prays lament, provides God's answer to Israel's long-
> prayed cries of lament, and guarantees the ultimate ces-
> sation of lament in the eschaton. Elsewhere in the New
> Testament, the church joins Jesus' laments in longing
> for the completion of what Jesus' ministry, death, and

12. Eklund, *Jesus Wept*, 12. Eklund cites Luke's downplay of emotions in
his portrayal of Jesus' prayer in Gethsemane as an example of Stoic influence.

13. Eklund, *Jesus Wept*, 12–14. Eklund notes that the fading use of lament
as protest is partially due to the theological emphasis on atonement, which
sees Jesus' lament only as "mourning over humanity's sin" (Eklund, *Jesus Wept*,
13). Patrick Miller argues to the contrary that Jesus' laments, and particularly
his cry of dereliction, indicate that he laments just as much over the suffering of humanity as he does over its sin (Patrick Miller, "Heaven's Prisoners:
The Lament as Christian Prayer," in Brown and Miller, *Lament*, 15–26). On
Paul's use and application of the lament psalms, Eklund notes, "Paul uses the
language of lament [in Ps 51] to build a case for the equal culpability of Jew
and Gentile before God, but also for God's faithfulness and justification of both
Jew and Gentile. By taking lines that originally referred to enemies or to the
wicked and applying them to all humanity, Paul has appropriated this part
of the lament pattern in order to indict sinful humanity and vindicate God's
righteousness." (Eklund, *Jesus Wept*, 13–14).

14. Eklund, *Jesus Wept*, 17.

resurrection began—the return of Christ and the consummation of God's kingdom.[15]

Although Jesus' life, death, and resurrection changed the face of lament, they did not remove it, but rather offered hope and joy bound up in eschatological yearning for Christ's glorious return. Given this reality, lament must be considered normative practice in individual and corporate worship, for it is in this way that the church joins together in the longing for the completion of Christ's redemptive work.

The following discussion of Eklund's theory of quotes or allusions of lament psalms, and also of the ethos of lament, sheds further light on the practice of corporate lament in the New Testament and the resulting implications for believers today.

"QUOTES OR ALLUSIONS" TO LAMENT PSALMS

Within the category of lament itself, echoes of the Psalms in the New Testament have been divided by Eklund into two subcategories: (1) texts that quote or allude to the lament psalms, and (2) texts that "evoke the ethos" of the Psalms.[16] Direct quotes or allusions to the Psalms are in the writings of Paul, Peter, John, and Hebrews and are especially found in the Gospels and in the words of Jesus, as discussed in chapter 2. The following exploration of echoes and extensions of the Psalms in the New Testament demonstrates the continued application of the well-known Old Testament language of lament by its authors. These echoes and extensions, bound up in the christological lens through which writers such as Paul, Peter, and John viewed their present suffering, can inform the corporate lament practices of modern believers. Representative examples from each of these authors are explored next.

---

15. Eklund, *Jesus Wept*, 17.
16. Eklund, *Jesus Wept*, 17–20.

The Lament Psalms in the Writings of Paul

Christians in the first century lived under Roman rule, and Paul often alluded to or referenced this—for example in his instruction on paying taxes to earthly rulers in Rom 13. Sylvia Keesmaat finds that the "tension" between "imperial justice and the justice of God" is noted throughout the letter and was a source of struggle and even persecution for the people.[17] Paul's opening statements in his letter to the Romans indicate his desire and passion for spreading the Gospel of Jesus Christ, of which he indicated in verses 16–17 that he was "not ashamed." The widely-held belief under claim by Roman rule that Caesar was the source of salvation through his military victories was boldly challenged in Paul's opening attribution of salvific power to Jesus Christ's gospel.[18]

According to Richard Hayes, Paul's allusion to Christ as the source of salvation of whom he is unashamed could have been rooted in Ps 71, which might account for Paul's terminology regarding shame.[19] Verses 1–2 (NRSV) sound the call for salvation from Yahweh alone: "In you, O LORD, I take refuge; let me never be put to shame. In your righteousness deliver me and rescue me; incline your ear to me and save me." Hays notes the parallel here between "righteousness" in verse 1 and "justice," which was likely the tone Paul drew from this psalm in what has been described as a challenge to the so-called sovereign rule of Caesar.[20] Similarly, Ps 62:1, and its claim of salvation in Yahweh alone, likely informed Paul's view of justice.

17. Sylvia C. Keesmaat, "Psalms in Romans and Galatians," in Moyise and Menken, 139–62.

18. Sylvia C. Keesmaat, "Psalms in Romans and Galatians," in Moyise and Menken, 139–62.

19. Hays, *Echoes of Scripture in the Letters of Paul*, 38.

20. Hays, *Echoes of Scripture in the Letters of Paul*, 38. Similarly, Craig Keener notes that throughout the letter, Paul connects Christ's salvific work on Calvary to the acquittal of these believers, further supporting his claim of Christ as ruler above Caesar: "Accusers raise accusations only at their own peril" in light of Christ's "vindication" and his subsequent exaltation to God's right hand. Keener, *Romans*, 111.

Given this call for God's justice in Rom 13:16–17, Keesmaat argues that Paul here "evoked the world of the lament, where the question of God's faithfulness and justice is up for grabs."[21] According to Keesmaat, the disorientation occurs as Paul points to the "radical dissonance" of Caesar's rule over against God's sovereignty, as he allows "the *question* of God's justice" to "whisper around the edges," echoing the fear of being put to shame in the face of Roman rule.[22] However, Paul's bold claim that he is "not ashamed" asserts to the Roman Christians that the sovereign God has indeed risen up and acted on their behalf. Keesmaat notes:

> And in asserting that he is *not* ashamed, Paul is thereby suggesting to his readers (hearers) that God *has* arisen, that God *has* acted according to his justice, that God *has* vindicated his people, and that *this* is the gospel, the good news that challenges the so-called "good news" of Rome.[23]

Finally, Paul strengthens his argument in support of salvation through the gospel of Jesus Christ, a salvation of which he is "not ashamed" (Rom 1:16–17 NRSV), with a possible allusion to Ps 98:2–3.[24] Here the psalmist references the righteousness/justice of God revealed to the nations: "The LORD has made known his victory; he has revealed his vindication in the sight of the nations. He has remembered his steadfast love and faithfulness to the house of Israel. All the ends of the earth have seen the victory of our God." Paul draws together the corporate body of Christ, beginning with the lament of Ps 71 and culminating with his confidence in the hope of salvation offered in Ps 98. Keesmaat sees Ps 98 as one of reorientation that has moved through lament and the cry for

21. Sylvia C. Keesmaat, "Psalms in Romans and Galatians," in Moyise and Menken, *Psalms*, 139–62.

22. Sylvia C. Keesmaat, "Psalms in Romans and Galatians," in Moyise and Menken, *Psalms*, 139–62, emphasis original.

23. Sylvia C. Keesmaat, "Psalms in Romans and Galatians," in Moyise and Menken, *Psalms*, 139–62, emphasis original.

24. Sylvia C. Keesmaat, "Psalms in Romans and Galatians," in Moyise and Menken, *Psalms*, 139–62.

salvation, and which ends in an acclamation of coming salvation for a world "created anew," even in the face of persecution.[25]

Among other references to the persecution of the Roman believers is the beloved and oft-quoted Rom 8 (NRSV). Developing his theme in this epistle of the superiority of Christ, Paul inserts allusions to and echoes of eschatological hope, while continuing to emphasize the justice of God against their persecutors.[26] To accomplish this, Paul weaves together the motifs of the "groaning" of creation (v. 22), the groaning of believers (v. 23), and that of God himself (v. 26):[27]

> For we know that the whole creation has been groaning in labor pains until now. And not only the creation, but we ourselves, who have the firstfruits of the Spirit, groan inwardly as we wait for adoption, the redemption of our bodies. For in hope we are saved. Now hope that is seen is not hope. For who hopes for what is seen? But if we hope for what we do not see, we wait for it with patience. Likewise the Spirit helps us in our weakness; for we do not know how to pray as we ought, but that very Spirit intercedes for us with sighs too deep for words.

The Greek word Paul uses for this groaning cry is the word predominantly used by the psalmists in their cries against their oppressors.[28] Keesmaat highlights this usage, stating, "This language originated in Israel's first experience of empire, and was repeatedly used when Israel found herself suffering under imperial control during her history."[29] The connection Paul draws here between Israel's groaning and that of the Roman believers brings to speech

25. Sylvia C. Keesmaat, "Psalms in Romans and Galatians," in Moyise and Menken, *Psalms*, 139–62.

26. Keener, *Romans*, 104.

27. Sylvia C. Keesmaat, "Psalms in Romans and Galatians," in Moyise and Menken, *Psalms*, 139–62.

28. Sylvia C. Keesmaat, "Psalms in Romans and Galatians," in Moyise and Menken, *Psalms*, 139–62. See Pss 18:7; 32:3; 69:4.

29. Sylvia C. Keesmaat, "Psalms in Romans and Galatians," in Moyise and Menken, *Psalms* 139–62. See Exod 2:23–24 and Lam 1:18, 21–22. For further in-depth discussion of Israel's groaning, see Keesmaat, *Paul and His Story*, 124–33.

the suffering of these first-century Christians, while connecting them to the hope that Christ identifies with them, stating in verse 26 (NRSV) that "the Spirit helps us in our weakness."

The conclusion of Rom 8 finds Paul quoting from Ps 44:22 (NRSV): "Because of you we are being killed all day long, and accounted as sheep for the slaughter." This cry to Yahweh for deliverance from oppression was likely known among many in Paul's audience, and its insertion here must have echoed their own desires for deliverance from persecution, along with their need for assurance of Christ's victory. It is here, according to Craig Keener, that Paul sounds the note of eschatological hope first introduced in Rom 8:23, with its emphasis on adoption and redemption.[30] Reinforcing his assertion, Paul asks, "If God is for us, who is against us?" (Rom 8:31 NRSV), once again using the image of the conqueror and connecting it to Christ in Rom 8:37 (NRSV): "No, in all these things we are more than conquerors through him who loved us." Keesmaat writes, "Paul is rejecting the imperial categories here of victory . . . and is replacing them with the category of suffering love."[31] Although their present circumstances indicated defeat, Paul announced that their suffering in solidarity would label them as members who could not be separated from the body of Christ.

The theme of Christians who, though now suffering, will ultimately be "more than conquerors" is a common one throughout Paul's writings, and especially in 2 Corinthians. Paul often mentioned his suffering and weakness throughout his letters and epistles as his means of identifying with the suffering of Christ.[32] In fact, Paul went as far as to state that suffering would be expected if one were to identify with a "rejected Messiah" and

30. Keener, *Romans*, 107. Hays believes Paul is drawing from the eschatological hope he believes is prophesied in Ps 44: "Scripture prophesies suffering as the lot of those . . . who live in the eschatological interval between Christ's resurrection and the ultimate redemption of the world." According to Hays, this is the vocational suffering of those who will be united with Christ. Hays, *Echoes of Scripture*, 58.

31. Sylvia C. Keesmaat, "Psalms in Romans and Galatians," in Schmutzer and Howard, *Psalms*, 139–62.

32. See for example 1 Cor 2:2; 2 Cor 4:10; Gal 2:20; Phil 3:7–11.

his "offensive Gospel."[33] Robert Plummer posits that this "fundamental Christological grounding of Christian suffering" is the foundation of the Christian calling to which Paul refers again and again throughout his writings.[34]

This central theme of Paul's writing, however, was turned against him by his adversaries, the "false apostles" in Corinth, who claimed Paul's apostleship was invalidated because it lacked "signs and wonders" in addition to his own healing and deliverance.[35] Given this extensive opposition, Paul spends much of 2 Corinthians making the case that "strength *in weakness*" is the greatest validation of the ministry of an apostle.[36] This point is perhaps most clearly expressed in 2 Cor 4:7–15, where Paul compares himself to an "earthen vessel" or ordinary clay pot in which a priceless treasure, the message of the Gospel, is being stored. Why would such a priceless treasure be stored in such an ordinary, even cracked pot such as Paul? So that it would be evident to all that "this extraordinary power belongs to God and does not come from us" (v. 7 NRSV).

In this key passage of 2 Cor 4:7–15, Paul once again calls on the Psalms to support his teaching about the paradoxical nature of suffering and new life in Christ. The parallel is found between verse 13 of Paul's text and Ps 116:10:

Ps 116:10	2 Cor 4:13
I kept my faith even when I said, "I am greatly afflicted."	But just as we have the same spirit of faith that is in accordance with scripture—"I believed and so I spoke"—we also believe and so we also speak.

Table 1. Parallels between Ps 116 and 2 Cor 4 (NRSV)

33. Plummer, "Role of Suffering," 8.

34. Plummer, "Role of Suffering," 8. See for instance Rom 8:17; 2 Cor 1:5; 2:14–15; Gal 6:12; Phil 3:10; Col 1:24–25.

35. Schreiner, *Paul*, 88, 94.

36. Schreiner, *Paul*, 88, 94, emphasis in original.

Like the psalmists, Paul vows to speak what he knows to be truth: the steadfast love of God has enabled him as well as them (both in the midst of their suffering and at its conclusion) to enter a place of new orientation brought about by the suffering. For the psalmists this is restoration to health and identification with the community, and for Paul, it is further identification with Christ.

Both Ps 116 and 2 Cor 4:7–15 are addressed to the community, of the psalmist or the church in Corinth, respectively. This communal element is key in that it calls on the community to share thanksgiving both in and for the suffering of each other.[37] Paul also makes an appeal toward the community of believers, reminding them that it is Christ who raises them out of their suffering so that they in turn might be examples of the newness of life given by grace through Christ.[38] In describing the mutual spiritual benefits between members of the body of Christ, Ernest Best notes that it is not only those who minister that share in the rejoicing and weeping, but also those members of the congregation who, in turn, build up those ministering.[39] In this way, the entire body, in enduring affliction, does not "lose heart" (v. 16 NRSV), but instead focuses on the renewal of the "inner nature" and the "eternal weight of glory beyond all measure" (v. 17 NRSV).

The Lament Psalms in 1 Peter.

The expectation articulated in the Epistles that believers would suffer is seen perhaps most clearly in 1 Peter, which was written to fellow Christians who were likely suffering persecution.[40] It is clearly more hortatory than expository in its purpose and tone, with its appeal for courage and steadfastness in the face of

37. Brueggemann and Bellinger note that the psalmist upbraids the community in Ps 116:11 (NRSV) for a seeming absence or lack of support during the time of disorientation: "I said in my consternation: everyone is a liar." Brueggemann and Bellinger, *Psalms*, 501.

38. Best, *Second Corinthians*, 43.

39. Best, *Second Corinthians*, 43.

40. McCartney, "Suffering in the Teaching of the Apostles," 108.

sometimes severe suffering.[41] Besides the suffering inflicted by slander and verbal abuse, the reference to "fiery ordeal" in 4:12 (NRSV) evoked the real possibility of physical harm and death, Hiebert notes.[42] Since the topic of suffering pervades the entire epistle, it was evidently intense, and thus Peter's central theme and concern. In order to address their suffering, Peter drew extensively on Pss 34 and 118, with several references to Isa 53 and the "suffering servant" language.[43] As in the writings of Paul, Peter addressed the community of believers as a whole, viewing their suffering as affecting not just individuals, but the entire body.

Peter's address to these believers reflects a radical transition in his perspective and relationship to Christ, McCartney points out. The same apostle who had initially rejected the fact that Christ should suffer (Mark 8:31–32) now embraces suffering with the understanding of its necessity in identifying with and becoming like Christ.[44] He goes so far as to call fellow believers to "rejoice insofar as you are sharing Christ's sufferings" (1 Pet 4:13 NRSV) because this is the measure of Christ's glory resting upon them. Earlier in the letter Peter wrote:

> For to this you have been called, because Christ also suffered for you, leaving you an example, so that you should follow in his steps. "He committed no sin, and no deceit was found in his mouth." When he was abused, he did not return abuse; when he suffered, he did not threaten, but entrusted himself to him who judges justly. (1 Pet 2:21–23 NRSV)

Here, Peter is recalling the suffering servant from Isa 53, and particularly the language of verse 9: "and there was no deceit in his mouth," which Peter uses in verse 22 (NRSV).[45]

Besides making extensive use of the suffering servant language of Isa 53, Peter also draws heavily on the psalms of lament

41. Hiebert, *First Peter*, 20.

42. Hiebert, *First Peter*, 20

43. Sue Woan, "Psalms in 1 Peter," in Moyise and Menken, *Psalms*, 213–30.

44. McCartney, "Suffering in the Teaching of the Apostles," 109.

45. Grudem, *I Peter*, 129.

and thanksgiving, especially Ps 34, in shaping his epistle.[46] He uses Ps 34 extensively throughout the epistle both as encouragement for believers, and to support his admonition to embrace sufferings in the name of Christ. Shown in table 2, Ps 34 is found in allusion or direct quotation in at least seven passages in 1 Peter.

Psalm 34 is significant and applicable to Peter's message in several ways. First, it is a psalm of deliverance or reorientation in which the psalmist boldly praises Yahweh for liberating him from "fears" and vows to "bless the LORD at all times." Although the psalm begins with the voice of the individual, it quickly takes on the communal tone in verse 3 (NRSV) when the psalmist declares, "O magnify the LORD with me, and let us exalt his name together." Brueggemann and Bellinger note that the call for communal participation is an invitation for others to take part in the individual's experience of deliverance, and in turn, to learn of the faithfulness of Yahweh.[47] Another important communal element of this psalm, according to Brueggemann and Bellinger, is that, in the Psalms, "seeking the Lord suggests cultic activity," and could indicate that the psalmist prayed in the temple during the crisis and prior to deliverance.[48] Now the psalmist crafts his thanksgiving into a lesson for the community regarding the faithfulness of Yahweh.

Psalm 34	Parallel Text	1 Peter	Parallel Text
34:4	"delivered me from all my fears"	3:6	"never let fears alarm you"
34:9	"fear the LORD"	1:15, 17	"live in reverent fear"

46. Wenham, *Psalms as Torah*, 186.
47. Brueggemann and Bellinger, *Psalms*, 169.
48. Brueggemann and Bellinger, *Psalms*, 169.

Psalm 34	Parallel Text	1 Peter	Parallel Text
34:13–17	"keep your tongue from evil and your lips from speaking deceit"	3:10–12	"let them keep their tongues from evil, and their lips from speaking deceit"
	"depart from evil . . . seek peace"		"turn away from evil . . . do good"
	"eyes of the LORD are on the righteous and his ears are open to their cry"		"eyes of the Lord are on the righteous, and his ears are open to their prayer"
	"the face of the LORD is against evildoers"		"the face of the Lord is against those who do evil"
34:14	"depart from evil and do good; seek peace and pursue it"	1:14	"do not be conformed to the desires you formerly had in ignorance"
34:13	"keep your tongue from evil and your lips from speaking deceit"	2:1	"rid yourselves, there-fore, of all malice and all guile, insincerity, envy, and all slander"
34:14	"depart from evil and do good; seek peace and pursue it"	2:12	"conduct yourselves honorably among the Gentiles"
34:14	"depart from evil and do good; seek peace and pursue it"	2:22; 3:9	"and no deceit was found in his mouth"
			"do not repay evil for evil, or abuse for abuse"

Table 2. Parallels and allusions between Ps 34 and 1 Peter (NRSV)[49]

49. Brueggemann and Bellinger, *Psalms*, 188–89; Sue Woan, "Psalms in 1 Peter," in Moyise and Menken, *Psalms*, 223–24.

Given the didactic nature of Ps 34, it is therefore not surprising that Peter would use much of it as the basis for his instruction to the suffering believers. His tone of encouragement to persecuted believers based on God's faithfulness to deliver parallels that of the psalm and in turn, calls the community to trust that he will sustain them. On this correlation between Ps 34 and Peter's epistle, Brueggemann and Bellinger note:

> The portrayal of the life of the righteous in these last verses [of Psalm 34] makes it clear that such a life is often found in the midst of suffering. The promise of Yahweh is not a promise of undisturbed happy circumstances but a promise of divine presence and hope in all of life. Verse 20 expresses this presence in a powerful way with the image of divine protection of "all their bones." The conclusion of the psalm is in a proverbial style affirming that those who take refuge in Yahweh will find redemption rather than condemnation.[50]

Given that the suffering of those to whom Peter wrote was extensive and ongoing, the use of Ps 34 is apropos in that it does not deny that suffering will happen. Instead, it calls believers as a community to expect and share in suffering, all the while clinging to the unmovable hope in verse 19 (NKJV): "Many are the afflictions of the righteous, but the Lord rescues them from them all."

Although not directly quoted by Peter, echoes of Ps 22 as well as of the suffering servant language of Isa 53 are heard in this epistle's opening verses. Peter's generic reference to "prophets" in verses 10–12, according to Hiebert, refers to a non-specific voice which looks forward to the future, instead of referencing a particular Old Testament prophet.[51] Here, Peter exhorts his readers to recall the many voices who predicted the sufferings of Christ, such as Isaiah in his description of the suffering servant in chapter 53, and possibly the prophecies concerning Christ in Ps 22. These voices predicted the manifold sufferings of Christ, some of which were relatable to Peter's audience. In calling the people to "look

50. Brueggemann and Bellinger, *Psalms*, 170.
51. Hiebert, *First Peter*, 63.

back" to these prophecies, Tim Keller maintains that Peter was reminding them that Christ was not indifferent to their suffering, but instead fully participated in it, even to a degree beyond which they would ever know.[52]

The Lament Psalms in Revelation

Steve Moyise notes the connection between Ps 137 and the narrative of Babylon's fall in Rev 18.[53] Psalm 137:9 (NRSV) finds the psalmist declaring to his Babylonian captors, "Happy shall they be who take your little ones and dash them against the rock." John alludes to this passage in Rev 18:6 (NRSV) where he records a voice from heaven declaring in reference to Babylon, "Render to her as she herself has rendered." Here, Moyise notes the use of similar verbs in the psalm and in Revelation in reference to the rendering of punishment to Babylon[54]: "John finds in Psalm 137 a graphic description of the fate of God's enemies, namely, that the punishment will fit the crime."[55] The central element of these two references is the prayer of imprecation by their author for vengeance, not by the people, but by God, who alone has authority to mete out judgment on the enemy.

Other echoes of the Psalms in Revelation include the expression of trust that concludes the communal lament found in Ps 106. Beginning as a hymn of praise, this psalm quickly changes direction, unfolding as a confession of sin as the writer recounts the narrative history of Israel.[56] As the psalmist pleads for help, he asks Yahweh to remember him (v. 4) and to show favor to the people

52. Keller, "Suffering."

53. Steve Moyise, "Psalms in the Book of Revelation," in Moyise and Menken, *Psalms*, 231–46.

54. Steve Moyise, "Psalms in the Book of Revelation," in Moyise and Menken, *Psalms*, 231–46. While the psalmist uses future and aorist tenses, John uses the imperative and aorist tenses.

55. Steve Moyise, "Psalms in the Book of Revelation," in Moyise and Menken, *Psalms*, 231–46.

56. Brueggemann and Bellinger, *Psalms*, 458.

in spite of their sinfulness (v. 5). Following this plea, the psalmist recounts the communal history of Israel's sinful deeds in breaking her covenant with Yahweh (vv. 6–46). Notable is the use of three specific verbs in reference to the sin of the people: "sinned," "committed iniquity," and "done wickedly," which show the pervasive and explicit nature of their sin.[57]

Given this central theme of remembrance, Brueggemann and Bellinger assert, it is likely that the psalmist is calling Israel to remember Yahweh's deliverance of the people from the oppression of Pharaoh.[58] Besides remembering his deliverance, the greater point of Ps 106 is the proclamation of Yahweh's mighty power among Israel and the surrounding nations (vv. 8, 47). This theme of remembrance is echoed and culminates in Rev 19:1–4, which records:

> After this I heard what seemed to be the loud voice of a great multitude in heaven, saying, "Hallelujah! Salvation and glory and power to our God, for his judgments are true and just; for he has judged the great whore who corrupted the earth with her fornication, and has avenged on her the blood of his servants." Once more they cried out, "Hallelujah! The smoke from her goes up forever and ever." And the twenty-four elders and the four living creatures fell down and worshipped God who is seated on the throne, saying, "Amen, Hallelujah!"

Moyise concludes that this praise of God for deliverance that culminates with "Amen, Hallelujah" echoes the concluding verses of Ps 106, which contains the singular occurrence of this identical phrase.[59] While noting that "Amen, Hallelujah" could have been a standard "liturgical repetition," Moyise notes that it is likely John was echoing this theme of thanksgiving following deliverance as found in this psalm.[60]

---

57. Brueggemann and Bellinger, *Psalms*, 459.

58. Brueggemann and Bellinger, *Psalms*, 459.

59. Steve Moyise, "Psalms in the Book of Revelation," Moyise and Menken, *Psalms*, 231–46.

60. Steve Moyise, "Psalms in the Book of Revelation," Moyise and Menken,

The multiple quotes or allusions to lament psalms found throughout the New Testament call believers to suffer so that they may be like Christ. Given the regular inclusion of such references, Dan McCartney goes so far as to claim that the "thesis" of the New Testament is that the suffering and death of Christ was the answer to the suffering and death of believers.[61]

FULFILLMENT OF THE OLD TESTAMENT REVERSAL THEME

However, in addition to this central thesis, another theme arises from the suffering and death of Christ: the hope in eschatological reversal, or the reversal of fortunes of the righteous and wicked, foretold in the Old Testament.[62] The teachings of Jesus throughout his lifetime were pervaded with this theme, although his actual methods were surprising, often countercultural, and even anticlimactic to his disciples and others who heard his teachings. Dan McCartney notes that this reversal was the heart of John the Baptist's question to Jesus in Matt 11:3 (NRSV): "Are you the one who is to come, or are we to wait for another?"[63] John's question was effectively asking about the reversal foretold in the Old Testament prophecies. Jesus replied that the reversal was already taking place because "the blind receive their sight and the lame walk, lepers are cleansed and the deaf hear, and the dead are raised up, and the poor have good news preached to them" (11:5).[64] That this reversal would be further accomplished through the suffering and death of

---

Psalms, 231–46.

61. Dan McCartney, "Suffering and the Goodness of God in the Gospels," in Morgan and Peterson, *Suffering and the Goodness*, 80–94.

62. Dan McCartney, "Suffering and the Goodness of God," in Morgan and Peterson, *Suffering and the Goodness*, 80–94. See for example Isa 9:6; Mic 5:5; Ezek 34:25–31; Zech 9:9–13.

63. Dan McCartney, "Suffering and the Goodness of God," in Morgan and Peterson, *Suffering and the Goodness*, 80–94.

64. Dan McCartney, "Suffering and the Goodness of God," in Morgan and Peterson, *Suffering and the Goodness*, 80–94.

Christ would come as a surprise even to John himself, as well as the other disciples.

Jesus would do more than suffer and die, however. He would "encompass" and redefine suffering in his death *and* in his resurrection, both for himself, his disciples, and finally for the whole world.[65] Jesus' all-encompassing resurrection would not only vindicate himself and his ministry over those who put him through humiliation and death, but would culminate in the vindication of all believers in the eschaton. Until that time, however, suffering was to be expected, as noted in Acts 14:22 (NRSV): "It is through many persecutions we must enter the kingdom of God."[66] Rebekah Eklund views the role of lament in the life of Jesus ultimately in light of his coming kingdom:

> New Testament lament trusts that God acts in the present through Jesus' resurrection and the sending of the Holy Spirit and that God will act in the future through the ultimate redemption and restoration of all creation. Jesus' proclamation of the kingdom and his death and resurrection signify the proleptic end of lament: Jesus prays lament, provides God's answer to Israel's long-prayed cries of lament and guarantees the ultimate cessation of lament in the eschaton.[67]

Jesus' death and resurrection did not remove the need to lament, but should rather be seen as the catalyst for lament in the New Testament and beyond.[68] Until eschatological hope is ultimately realized, believers cry out in their suffering, held in the tension of the "already-and-not-yet," as their laments echo with the cry, "Thy kingdom come."

65. Dan McCartney, "Suffering and the Goodness of God," in Morgan and Peterson, *Suffering and the Goodness*, 80–94.

66. Dan McCartney, "Suffering and the Goodness of God," in Morgan and Peterson, *Suffering and the Goodness*, 80–94.

67. Eklund, *Jesus Wept*, 17.

68. Eklund, *Jesus Wept*, 17.

THE "ETHOS" OF THE LAMENT PSALMS

Many New Testament narrative texts are not directly modeled on psalmic lament, but "evoke the ethos" of lament, i.e., embody the spirit of laments found in the Psalms, according to Eklund.[69] While pleas for help in the Psalms were directed to Yahweh, in the Gospels such petitions were directed toward Jesus Christ.[70] Table 3 illustrates examples found throughout Matthew, Mark, and Luke that mirror the plea for mercy commonly found throughout the psalms of lament:

Narrative	Matthew	Mark	Luke
Jesus awakens and calms the storm	8:23–27	4:35–41	—
Peter's cry while walking on water	14:22–33	—	—
Two blind men cry out for restored sight	9:27–31	—	—
Cry of the Canaanite woman	15:21–28	7:24–30	—
Demon-possessed boy	17:14–28	—	—
Two blind men on road to Jericho	20:29–34	—	—
Blind Bartemaeus	—	10:46–52	—
Ten lepers	—	—	17:11–19
Blind man on the road	—	—	18:35–43

Table 3. Pleas for help in the Gospels

Consistent in the previous passages is the cry "Have mercy on me," or some variation of this plea based on the particular context. This cry resonates throughout the psalms of disorientation, and

69. Eklund, *Jesus Wept*, 17.
70. Eklund, *Jesus Wept*, 17.

could have found its source there given the use of the Psalms for individual and corporate worship by the Jewish community.

The account of Jesus and the disciples in the storm at sea, although presented as a narrative, is a New Testament text which can be read as moving through Brueggemann's "cycle" of orientation, disorientation, and new orientation in a pattern similar to that of the lament psalms. Mark 4:35–42 (NRSV) gives the account:

> On that day, when evening had come, he said to them, "Let us go across to the other side." And leaving the crowd, they took him with them in the boat, just as he was. And other boats were with him. And a great windstorm arose, and the waves beat into the boat, so that the boat was already being swamped. But he was in the stern, asleep on the cushion. And they woke him and said to him, "Teacher, do you not care that we are perishing?" And he woke up and rebuked the wind and said to the sea, "Peace! Be still!" Then the wind ceased, and there was a dead calm. He said to them, "Why are you afraid? Have you still no faith?" And they were filled with great fear and said to one another, "Who then is this, that even the wind and the sea obey him?"

Prior to this account in Mark 4, Jesus shared several parables with the crowds and then privately with his disciples, sharing deeper spiritual truths for those who could hear and understand. Following his long day of teaching, Jesus had requested that the disciples go with him to the other side of the lake (v. 35), presumably to do more teaching, healing, or other types of ministry. At the onset of the storm, the disciples move into a state of disorientation during which they voiced fear and distress as they cried out for Jesus to save them (v. 38). The cry of the disciples, which questions Jesus' care and concern (v. 38), echoes the expressions of abandonment found at times in the psalms of lament.[71] Psalm

71. Scott Ellington notes that, although questions of "why?" and "how long?" are often missing from New Testament laments, invocations, pleas, and complaints comprise the primary types of petitions found there. Ellington finds in the disciples' cry, "Lord, save us! We are perishing!" recorded in Matt 8:25, a combination of the invocation, plea, and complaint in one succinct and

77:8–9 (NRSV) finds the psalmist asking, "Has his steadfast love ceased forever?" and "Has God forgotten to be gracious?" These and similar questions echo throughout the psalms of lament, demonstrating a universal cry for deliverance in times of disorientation. Matthew's account of this story finds the disciples rousing Jesus from sleep with the petition in 8:25 (NRSV): "Lord, save us! We are perishing!" Although Matthew's account, with its cry of distress, differs in tone from the complaint found in Mark's Gospel, the sentiment is the same: "Save us Lord, or we will die." This is the cry of disorientation so familiar to the psalmists.

Rebekah Eklund notes that in this passage, the disciples directly echo the cry in Ps 107:25, 29 (NRSV), which states, "For he commanded and raised the stormy wind, which lifted up the waves of the sea. . . . He made the storm be still, and the waves of the sea were hushed."[72] Psalm 107:30 (NRSV) goes on to note the response recorded by the psalmist: "Then they were glad because they had quiet, and he brought them to their desired haven." The cry of the disciples in both Gospel accounts awakens Jesus who immediately speaks to the storm, commanding it to become peaceful and still (Mark 4:39; Matt 8:26). Immediately, at Jesus' rebuke of the storm, the state of new orientation is established as the disciples experienced yet another dimension of Jesus' identity they had not previously known.[73] The cry once directed to Yahweh is now directed to Jesus Christ as the disciples come to more clearly understand his divine nature.

The account of the Canaanite or Syro-Phoenecian woman found in Matt 15:21–38 and Mark 7:24–30 is an example of a narrative lament. Matthew's Gospel gives the following account in 15:21–28 (NRSV):

> Jesus left that place and went away to the district of Tyre and Sidon. Just then a Canaanite woman from that region came out and started shouting, "Have mercy on me, Lord, Son of David; my daughter is tormented by a

---

urgent request. Ellington, *Risking Truth*, 166.

72. Eklund, *Jesus Wept*, 19.

73. Ellington, *Risking Truth*, 166.

demon." But he did not answer her at all. And his disciples came and urged him, saying, "Send her away, for she keeps shouting after us." He answered, "I was sent only to the lost sheep of the house of Israel." But she came and knelt before him, saying, "Lord, help me." He answered, "It is not fair to take the children's food and throw it to the dogs." She said, "Yes, Lord, yet even the dogs eat the crumbs that fall from their master's table." Then Jesus answered her, "woman, great is your faith! Let it be done for you as you wish." And her daughter was healed instantly.

Within this story, four common elements of the lament psalms can be found, including (1) the address ("Lord, Son of David"), (2) the complaint ("my daughter is tormented by a demon"), (3) the plea ("Have mercy on me"), and (4) the motivational statement ("even the dogs eat the crumbs that fall from their master's table"). Ellington also notes the "divine contribution" found both in this New Testament lament and many psalms, which he describes as "the silence of God."[74] Jesus' initial lack of response and the woman's continued complaint recorded in Matthew's Gospel form the heart of this story and propel it to its final resolution, the healing of the daughter. Jesus' words to the woman function as a "salvation oracle," turning her cry from "plea to praise," and from "despair to hope."[75]

The narratives of the disciples' cry to Jesus during the storm and of the Canaanite woman's plea for deliverance represent a continuation of Old Testament lament prayer in the New Testament. These representative stories show not only that lament continued, but that honest, heartfelt dialogue was welcomed and responded to by God himself. These narrative laments and the personal laments of Jesus fulfilled, in part, the prophecy of Isa 53:3 (NRSV) that Jesus was a "man of suffering and acquainted with infirmity," his own and that of others. Luke 4:18–19 (NRSV) records Jesus, reading from

74. Ellington, *Risking Truth*, 178. The absence or silence of God is noted throughout the psalms of lament. See for example Pss 22:1; 10:1; 13:1; 55:1–2; 69:16–17; 88:1–2, 14; 102:1–2. Ps 51:9, 11 records David pleading for God not to hide his face, nor to be cast from the presence of God.

75. O'Day, "Surprised by Faith," 294.

the scroll of Isaiah and referring to himself as the one who was anointed to "bring good news to the poor . . . proclaim release to the captives and recovery of sight to the blind . . . to let the oppressed go free." This mission, prophesied in Isaiah, would ultimately lead Jesus to the fulfillment of Isaiah's prophecy of his own suffering in Isa 53, and demonstrate the fulfillment in his earthly ministry, but his own suffering, death, and resurrection would forever change the meaning of believers' suffering for all time.

CONCLUSION

The clear echoes and extensions of psalmic lament in the New Testament, as well as of other passages that reflect more broadly the ethos of lament, demonstrate the ongoing need for the church to know and understand the rich language of suffering found in the Psalms. Given that much of the New Testament was written to the persecuted church, it is easy to hear these echoes throughout the letters and epistles. The epistle writers sought not only to give language for expressing lament, but also to gather up the suffering of believers in the work of the crucified Christ and the eschatological hope that resulted from his identification with their suffering. The writer to the Hebrews captured this hope in 4:15–16 (NRSV), stating, "For we do not have a high priest who is unable to sympathize with our weaknesses, but we have one who in every respect has been tested as we are, yet without sin."

Christ's use of the lament psalms identified him as this very high priest, the *Christus dolor*, who modeled the truth that the road to praise and new orientation could only be reached by passing through the sorrow and lament of disorientation. His death and resurrection became the template for the lives of all believers, and proved that though suffering is unavoidable, it is bound up in the eschatological hope given by the *Christus victor*. He also modeled that the very genuineness of praise and the glory of new orientation and resurrection could not be fully felt without the ugliness of the cry of lament.

The models of lament found in the Psalms, Christ's prayers, and the New Testament writers' theology of suffering are foundational for modern corporate worship practices.

5

Implications for Corporate Worship

Where lament is absent, covenant comes into being only as a celebration of joy and well-being . . . Since such a celebrative, consenting silence does not square with reality, covenant minus lament is finally a practice of denial, cover-up, and pretense, which sanctions social control.

—WALTER BRUEGGEMANN[1]

THIS BOOK HAS EXAMINED the centrality of the psalms, including the lament psalms, in the worship of ancient Israel, their presence in the prayers of Christ, and their impact in shaping a theology of suffering and lament in the Gospels and Epistles in the New Testament. Chapter 2 demonstrated the integral use of the lament psalms in both individual and corporate worship in Israel, focusing on the dialogical nature of Israel's relationship with Yahweh, and the faithful expressions of suffering which predominate the Psalter. Chapter 3 examined Jesus' use of the lament psalms in his prayers. Finally, chapter 4 explored the use of the lament psalms across the

1. Brueggemann, *Psalms and the Life of Faith*, 68.

New Testament—their presence in the Gospels, and in the writings of Paul, Peter, and John.

The preceding chapters aimed to show that the psalms function throughout the biblical canon as models for worship, and as such serve as important templates for current planners and leaders of corporate worship. Examination of the various genres of the Psalms yields clear and definite implications for soul care in the evangelical church. One such implication which has been consistently central to corporate worship is that God is to be praised, and that the gathered church should celebrate and offer thanksgiving for Christ's gift of redemption through his death on the cross and resurrection. While this premise for offering praise is vital for corporate worship, of equal importance is the need for corporate worship to be a safe place in which believers can cry out as did the psalmists when life experience and belief come into conflict. An undeniable precedent for lament as worship is consistently present throughout Scripture, as demonstrated in preceding chapters.

What, then, should be the response to those suffering within the corporate body? How may those in church leadership better plan for and minister to worshipers who would cry out as the psalmist, "How long, O LORD?" The body of Christ has been wondrously gifted and equipped with professionals and scholars from across disciplines, all of whom can and should contribute through their various ministries to the care of souls. In 1 Cor 12:6 (NRSV), Paul reminds believers that though there is a variety of gifts, they come from the same Spirit who "activates all of them." He continues in verse 7 (NRSV): "To each is given the manifestation of the Spirit for the common good." Paul goes on to explain that God has specifically placed all parts of the body in relation to one another in order that there be "no dissention within the body, but the members may have the same care for one another" (v. 25 NRSV). Paul's body metaphor for the church demonstrates, therefore, the vitality and necessity of all members fully and faithfully functioning together.

The overarching purpose of this book has been to bring attention to the needs of believers for soul care across the body of

Christ, specifically the bringing of those needs into corporate worship, and to encourage utilization of the multitude of ministries in Christ's body to better meet the needs. Attitudes within some sectors of Christianity toward counseling as a profession and an essential ministry of the church have often been resistant or skeptical in past decades. The crying needs inside and outside the church in the present day demand that all ministries of the church partner together to serve the "common good" of the suffering. Such joint ministry is not an option, but a necessity in current culture.

This chapter first presents a summary of conclusions and undergirding premises drawn from the examination of Scripture in the preceding chapters that speak to the need for soul care across the spectrum of needs. The chapter concludes with foundational considerations for implementing these premises into corporate worship practices.

CONCLUSIONS AND UNDERGIRDING PREMISES

From the voice of Abel's blood crying out to God, to the protests of the psalmists, to Christ's anguished prayer in the garden of Gethsemane, and the cry of martyrs in Revelation, tears and prayers of suffering are found across the canon. While Scripture makes it clear that Christ's sacrificial death triumphed over evil and suffering (Col 2:13–15) giving believers cause to rejoice, it also makes clear that suffering and "various trials" (1 Pet 1:6 NRSV) will continue to be normative until Christ's return. We may conclude, then, that if we follow the biblical example, we will weep.

Thus, the wonder of Scripture, as explored in chapters 2 through 4 of this book, comes in part from the fact that it "addresses the world as we know it," according to Timothy Land and Paul Tripp, and paints a clear picture of God as intimately interested and involved in the details of life, in sorrow as well as in rejoicing.[2] Central to this picture are the psalms of lament which involve real people wrestling with God and asking aggressive questions in the

2. Lane and Tripp, *How People Change*, 96.

midst of their suffering. This clear picture is often vastly different from that of modern evangelical corporate worship which tends to emphasize rejoicing and positive thinking. Alternatively, the psalms paint a vastly different picture of the mixture of sorrow and rejoicing, of protest and praise. Instead of an unrealistic emphasis on perfection, the psalms, according to John Witvliet, demonstrate a balance of "tenacious faith" and "candid grappling," a consistent movement through the cycle of orientation and disorientation.[3]

From the Scriptures, therefore, can be distilled at least six undergirding principles on which to build a theology of suffering and corporate soul care:

1. The psalms are God's "case book" of soul care. The prayers in the Psalms represent all conditions of the human heart and as such, serve as exemplars for the processing of all human emotions.[4]

2. Worship is not pain denial. The psalmic laments legitimize protest and complaint as valid forms of prayer, and acts of faith and trust.[5]

3. Worship is *dialogical* and *relational*. The relational nature of worship presupposes the use of expressions from across the spectrum of human emotions.

4. Worship is ultimately communal. Although the psalms of lament are predominantly written by individuals, they ultimately view suffering as communal, given the centrality of the community to the well-being of the individual.

5. Lament fuels authentic praise.

6. Lament has an eschatological dimension. Christ's crucifixion transforms lament into an eschatological practice as it accelerates the consummation of Christ's ministry.[6]

---

3. Witvliet, *Worship Seeking Understanding*, 40.

4. Keller, "Praying the Gospel."

5. Runck, conversation with author, April 12, 2014.

6. Ellington, *Risking Truth*, 181.

These undergirding principles and their implications for modern corporate worship are briefly examined next.

The Psalms as God's "Case Book"

The beautiful poetry of the Psalms was written by real people who lived and worshiped in ancient Israel. Although the circumstances of their lives were much different from ours today, their humanity—its joys, sorrows, victories, and losses—was the same. According to Tim Keller, therefore, the psalms function as God's "case book" of prayers prayed from across the emotional spectrum. As such, they teach us to pour out our emotions "pre-reflectively," that is, to pray our emotions first, before filtering them, to lay the emotions bare in the presence of God, the only true source of healing wholeness.[7]

There are at least two main implications of these myriad expressions for modern corporate worship. First, planners and leaders of worship must be sensitive to the needs and life circumstances of those whom they shepherd and plan the corporate service appropriately. Thus, for example, a service of exuberant rejoicing following the sudden death of a child in the church community would not only be insensitive but would greatly hinder both the bereaved family and the larger corporate body from bringing their pain into worship and processing it in the presence of God. Sensitive planning and leading, therefore, teaches us that the corporate gathering is a safe place to bring our sorrows, and that we may enter into God's presence and pray pre-reflective prayers, whether using the words of the psalmists or our own. Making space for such reflection requires careful teaching, planning, and modeling of lament prayers by those in leadership so that those who are suffering can feel greater freedom to express their own lament before God. Nancy Duff suggests that opportunities for corporate lament should be introduced in a similar manner as regular times

---

7. Keller, "Praying Your Tears."

of confession and repentance in order to make lament a corporate practice with which we would be comfortable.[8]

In addition to the work needed by planners and leaders of corporate worship, the expertise of professional counselors and social workers in the congregation should be utilized. The drawing together of the various ministries within the corporate body can better equip the pastoral and worship leadership within the church to lead those who are suffering in prayers of lament. By utilizing and drawing upon the expertise and input of those who are professionally trained in soul care, those who lead in song selection and service planning in corporate worship can more effectively and sensitively compose prayers of lament, and can choose songs and scripture readings that teach others to honestly and courageously name their feelings in God's presence.[9]

WORSHIP IS NOT PAIN DENIAL

Praise is a central element of corporate worship mandated by Scripture. Yet, worship that does not also include space for expressions of lament can not only become unbalanced, according to Duff, but even "self-deceptive" and devoid of hope.[10] While praise of God is mandated in Scripture (e.g., Pss 95, 98, 150), we must realize that praise does not guarantee hope, nor does lament negate it. The common misconception is that only praise can be connected to faith and hope. This misconception stereotypes lament as negative thinking and as a practice to be avoided. Clinton McCann cites this misconception as the reason for the limited number of lament psalms and hymns found in most corporate worship services today.[11] Their absence results in a hymnody that is at best one-sided, and at worst misrepresentative of a life equally marked by orientation and disorientation. With respect to such "one-sided"

8. Duff, "Recovering Lamentation," 8–9.

9. Duff, "Recovering Lamentation," 9.

10. Duff, "Recovering Lamentation," 4.

11. McCann, *Theological Introduction*, 85.

hymnody, Brueggemann writes, "It is very clear that a church that goes on singing 'happy songs' in the face of raw reality is doing something very different from what the Bible itself does."[12] Instead, corporate worship practices should strive to reflect the balance in the Psalms, a balance that does not deny suffering but offers it as an honest and authentic act of worship.

Corporate worship that includes only positive expressions to the exclusion of lament inaccurately associates lament with negative thinking. Such worship also faces the danger of directing our confidence to self instead of its rightful place in God alone. A worship experience that connects faith and praise to positive thinking, in which we challenge one another to think enough positive thoughts until the suffering ceases, would be foreign to the psalmists. Such encouragement to simply think positive thoughts, according to Glenn Pemberton, results in confidence that has "replaced recognition of need."[13] Pemberton cites Jesus' own transparent modeling of lament within a group setting at the death of Lazarus:

> When Jesus encountered grieving sisters, contemplated his own impending death, or hung on a cross, he did not try to comfort everyone by telling them to have more faith, that God has a plan, or not to worry because "all things work together for the good of those who love the Lord." He did not lead them in a song of praise—*he lamented*—not for lack of faith or doubt in the Father, but because of his faith and because of his relationship with a Father who understands life at sea.[14]

The decision to bring his pain to God was an authentic act of worship that represents a turning away from human hubris and pride to an acknowledgement that God alone can save.

---

12. Brueggemann, *Message of the Psalms*, 52.
13. Pemberton, *Hurting with God*, 40.
14. Pemberton, *Hurting with God*, 52, emphasis original.

WORSHIP IS DIALOGICAL AND RELATIONAL

In chapter 2 we explored the dialogical nature of Israel's relationship with God. Relationships devoid of dialogue, or those that embody only positive expressions are relationships that are one-sided, and ultimately unhealthy. As previously noted, the psalms are pre-reflective prayers spoken directly *to* God, as opposed to prayers or songs *about* God. Such direct discourse—both as praise and lament—establishes or confirms the relationship between the psalmist and God.

This dialogical model found in the Psalms has important implications for modern corporate worship practices. The psalmists understood that their relationship with God was all-encompassing, and as such, included all of life experience. Brueggemann has explained that the psalmists teach believers that "there is nothing out of bounds, nothing precluded or inappropriate [to express to God]," and to "withhold parts of life . . . is in fact to withhold part of life from the sovereignty of God."[15] Thus, a balanced and rich variety of expressions in corporate worship serves to deepen and strengthen the relationship between God and individual worshipers, and between individuals and the worshiping community as a whole.

LAMENT AS AN ACT OF COMMUNITY

The Psalms, even when written from the viewpoint of the individual, often ended in either an affirmation of God's faithfulness to the community (Ps 22:25) or with the psalmist mourning his marginalized state (Ps 42:4). Feelings of marginalization caused by suffering are a reality for many and are augmented by the individualistic nature of the current culture. One vital function of corporate worship, therefore, is to restore the element of community as God's people so familiar to the psalmists. Paul's use of the "body" (1 Cor 12) and "building" (Eph 2) metaphors resonates with this sense of community and appeal to us in a countercultural call to focus on our corporate identity as a unified body. Such practices

15. Brueggemann, *Message of the Psalms*, 52.

encourage us to be bearers of hope for those who cannot find hope within themselves.[16]

While individual laments predominate in the Psalter, the corporate laments are equally as important as templates for corporate worship. These laments (e.g., Pss 44, 74, 79, 137), when read in community, remind us that we are "citizens," and caution against the indifference endemic to the individualistic culture. Additionally, these corporate laments, such as Ps 74, can be prayed by the congregation as a means to grieve for those who are persecuted worldwide. In this way, the psalms serve as both template for and teacher of prayer, bringing the community into greater solidarity with brothers and sisters across the world.[17]

Outside the Psalms, the lament as an act of community is also found in the writings of Paul. In what is perhaps his clearest admonition on the subject, Paul admonished believers in Rom 12:15: "Rejoice with those who rejoice, weep with those who weep." There was no delineation between rejoicing and weeping, nor indication that one was communal and the other relegated to the small group or private therapy session. Paul's command was clear: both rejoicing and weeping should be done in community.

LAMENT FUELS AUTHENTIC PRAISE

In chapter 2 we discussed the cycle often found in the psalms of lament to praise, or disorientation to new orientation, and the repetition of that cycle. Psalm 138, for example, demonstrates that praise is robust and meaningful when fueled by the remembrance of deliverance: "On the day I called, you answered me; you increased my strength of soul" (v. 3 NRSV); "For though the LORD is high, he regards the lowly" (v. 6a NRSV); and "Though I walk in

16. Duff, "Recovering Lamentation," 4.

17. Pemberton asks important questions regarding the need for solidarity across the worldwide body of Christ: "Why do our hymnals portray Christianity as a celebration of one victory after another while neglecting voices crying out from the margins of loss and defeat? Is this portrayal true to our world? Is it true to biblical theology?" Pemberton, *Hurting with God*, 40.

the midst of trouble, you preserve me against the wrath of my ene-mies" (v. 7a NRSV). These recollections of times of suffering and of God's deliverance lead the psalmist to offer thanks with his "whole heart" (v. 1 NRSV), to "bow down toward your holy temple" (v. 2 NRSV), and to proclaim his praise so profoundly that "all the kings of the earth shall praise you" (v. 4 NRSV). The psalmist offered profound, exuberant praise, the kind that could only come from the recollection of deep sorrow out of which God delivered him.

Gerald Peterman, commenting on the unique nature of praise born of lament, goes so far as to claim, "Without pain, praise is 'thin' and halfhearted."[18] Practically, planners and leaders of corporate worship can aid in the understanding of this cycle by organizing services around themes of the church calendar during times such as Holy Week. While the rejoicing and praise associ-ated with Easter Sunday is merited, it can only be fully felt after we have first journeyed through the lament of the events of Christ's passion associated with the days prior, with weeping, crucifixion, and death. Only as we are led through the sorrow of Christ's suf-fering and death can the magnificence, beauty, and power of his resurrection begin to be comprehended and be fully celebrated.

LAMENT AS ESCHATOLOGICAL PRACTICE

The death and resurrection of Christ propelled his followers into a consistent tension between rejoicing born of redemption and the cry, "Come, Lord Jesus!" (Rev 22:20 NRSV). The eschatological function of lament directly contradicts the triumphalist philosophy that seeks to achieve freedom from sorrow in the present, claiming that Christ's promise of abundant life (John 10:10) meant that the dissonance of suffering would be removed, or that it would have lit-tle impact on the Christian. Instead, lament acknowledges the pres-ent reality of the brokenness of fallen humanity in a fallen world, holding these in tension with the hope of God's coming kingdom.

18. Andrew Schmutzer, "Longing to Lament: Returning to the Language of Suffering," in Peterman and Schmutzer, *Between Pain and Grace*, 103–30.

This tension, perhaps it can be said, is the beauty of lament, as it resists the present suffering while reaching forward in hope.

While it has been posited that suffering must be given voice in the gathered church, and that we must share in the communal cry of lament, it must also be emphasized that lament is not the final word. Ultimately, lament for the Christian will end in praise, as it did in nearly all the psalms. The offering of praise to God, according to John Swinton, enables believers to "take seriously the pain and sadness of the world, but refuse to be crushed by it."[19] However, even heartfelt praise, offered by believers in thankfulness unto God, somehow does not satisfy the longing of those still living with unanswered questions in a broken world.

Thus, it is important for worship leaders to hold in tension the triumph of Christ's sacrificial love with his ultimate coming defeat of death and the hope that brings.[20] In short, expressions of suffering and lament in corporate worship cannot be divorced from the cry in Rev 22:20 (NRSV), "Come, Lord Jesus." While the theme of suffering due to persecution pervades the New Testament, so does the cry for Christ's kingdom to come. Though not all suffer from persecution, life in a fallen and sinful world will bring suffering and sorrow, and will always lead us to cry out for Christ's return. "Following Christ's ascension," worship scholar Matthew Westerholm writes, "the church lives in the days when the bridegroom has been taken away from them (Matt 9:15). This is a season to lament."[21]

In addressing the Roman believers, Paul reminds them that "we boast in our hope of sharing the glory of God. And not only that, but we also boast in our sufferings" (Rom 5:2–5 (NRSV)). Douglas Hall comments, "Paul knows that 'the story, as yet, has no ending,' or to be more accurate, he knows that the ending (*eschatos*) . . . is a matter of hope, not of sight, and as such, an ending *out of* and *towards which* we are commanded to live."[22] The unfinished

19. Swinton, *Raging with Compassion*, 113.

20. Beker, *Suffering and Hope*, 97.

21. Westerholm, "'Hour Is Coming and Is Now Here,'" 190.

22. Hall, *God and Human Suffering*, 143.

"story" in which we now live necessarily holds the tension of both sorrow and hope. If the corporate worship service is comprised of only praise and thanksgiving it will ultimately leave the suffering feeling as outsiders, and it will not be faithful to the model found in the Psalms. Giving believers space and the means of expressing sorrow and lament, using the broad range of emotions found in the Psalms, comforts the sorrowful until the coming of Christ's kingdom.

FOUNDATIONAL CONSIDERATIONS FOR FACILITATING LAMENT IN CORPORATE EVANGELICAL WORSHIP

The promise of redemption and the hope of the coming of Christ's kingdom is today more urgent that ever in the post-9/11 world where suffering and persecution are the daily reality for many Christians. While North American believers are largely exempt from persecution, Christians in areas such as North Korea, the Middle East, and North Africa suffer for their faith on a daily basis.[23] While suffering and persecution may ebb and flow, the laments of the psalmists and those of first-century believers continue, even though the triumphalism of North American culture often silences their expression.[24] Thus, it is important for worship

23. "World Watch List."

24. C. Clifton Black reminds believers that the long line of those who lament continues and connects to the psalmists as well as to first-century believers addressed by Paul and others: "As long as we live with God in a world destined for glory yet still unredeemed, at times unspeakably blasphemed, we shall lament even as we rejoice." Black carefully cautions Christian leadership to note the difference between grief and lament: "Well-intentioned but mistaken psychotherapists have confused grief with lament, implying that lamentation expresses a definable stage in a predictable grieving process. A person or family proceeds through 'stages of grief,' which, if executed successfully . . . eventuate in a mentally reconstituted individual or group. . . . This I know, by faith, and from experience: grief may wane or become numbed, but lament is not a 'stage' from which children destined for the glory of God evolve, then leave behind (Col. 1:24–29)." Thus, since life is consistently intertwined with suffering, space for it in the liturgy must be consistent. Black, "Persistence of

leaders to attend prayerfully and intentionally to the needs of the suffering within their congregations, as well as those in the world-wide community of believers. As modeled by Paul and other writers of the New Testament, celebration of Christ's triumph must be held in tension with the acknowledgement of present suffering. Without this tension, according to Beker, either suffering is devoid of hope and results in despair and despondency or hope apart from suffering becomes fallacious and baseless.[25] The careful and prayerful interweaving of these varied elements into the liturgy must acknowledge the suffering of local believers and the larger persecuted church, while undergirding these realities with proclamation of the hope and redemption given through the gospel and the promise of Christ's coming reign.

The following elements provide a solid foundation for a worship service that can sustain this tension biblically: (1) a clear theology of the cross, (2) relearning and reclaiming the language of lament, and (3) regular recital and sharing of the common story or shared history of the church body.

A CLEAR THEOLOGY OF THE CROSS

In his article "The Friday Voice of Faith," Walter Brueggemann states, "The loss of the lament psalm in the worship life of the church is essentially the loss of a theology of the cross."[26] The cross paradoxically teaches us that strength is found in weakness, and that resurrection cannot take place without death, and the accompanying tears and suffering. Christ's suffering shows us that he is able to "sympathize with our weaknesses" (Heb 4:15 NRSV). Taking appropriate time to linger in the lament in corporate worship without pressure of an immediate rush to rejoicing reminds us that Christ understands human frailty, and that we can safely bring suffering to the cross within the community of believers.

---

the Wounds," 53.

25. Beker, *Suffering and Hope*, 31–38.

26. Brueggemann, "Friday Voice of Faith."

While the paradox of the cross seems to be largely rejected in triumphalist North American culture, the Christian church dare not reject it. Echoing Beker's connection of suffering to hope, Brueggemann envisions the relationship between lament and praise as the "Friday and Sunday of Christian faith," respectively, and sees in it the pattern of crucifixion and resurrection modeled in the sufferings and ultimate triumph of Christ.[27] By implication, to remove the acknowledgment of suffering and to focus only on the triumph of Christ's resurrection is to lose an entire dimension of the meaning of Christ's salvific work. While Christ did indeed triumph over sin and death, he did not do so apart from the suffering of the cross. Thus, while a triumph-intoxicated church will much more easily embrace Christ's resurrection and finds comfort in celebrating, an important dimension of this triumph is lost when we do not invest time weeping over the pain of his death.

While Christ's triumph over death is the turning point of all time and the source of the Christian's hope, his suffering and death is something of which we must regularly be reminded. The psalms of lament can facilitate this reminder, or in the very least, serve as templates for new songs of corporate lament. These types of expressions not only help worshipers process their personal suffering, but can enable them to both receive and share Christ's compassion and mercy with believers locally and worldwide. If lament is to be restored, worship leaders and planners must assist those they serve in a renewed understanding of and love for the cross.

RELEARNING AND RECLAIMING
THE LANGUAGE OF LAMENT

The focus of this book has been on the biblical foundations for the musical portion of corporate worship, finding much of its basis in the psalms of lament. Incorporation of lament into corporate worship, however, can be accomplished through any of our liturgical

---

27. Brueggemann, "Friday Voice of Faith."

practices, including prayers, the reading of Psalms, corporate music, art, and preaching.

Structuring the language of worship to encourage specific kinds of laments is work which must be carefully, and prayerfully completed. Historically, lament in the liturgy has focused almost exclusively on penitence and confession.[28] The Seven Penitential Psalms, chosen by Augustine, eventually came to be linked to a specific "cardinal sin": (1) Ps 6: anger; (2) Ps 32: pride; (3) Ps 38: gluttony; (4) Ps 51: lechery; (5) Ps 102: greed; (6) Ps 130: envy; and (7) Ps 143: sloth.[29] According to Peterman, these psalms eventually became the focus of corporate lament, to the near-exclusion of other expressions in public worship, with the exception of special services.[30] However, given that some suffering is undeserved, and not the result of sin, the broad range of emotions expressed across the psalms of lament, not only the penitential psalms, must become part of the language of the church.

Finally, when modeled on the prayers of the psalmists, corporate lament often eventually culminates in an expression of confidence in God's faithfulness and steadfast love.[31] Space and time for such expressions during the corporate service must be included. Singer-songwriter and author, Michael Card, in his 2005 book *A Sacred Sorrow: Reaching Out to God in the Lost Language of Lament*, established a turning point in evangelical awareness of the need for lament in corporate worship. Writing to the church after 9/11, Michael Card proclaims as a central theme in the book that song "born in the wilderness of suffering" is ultimately the truest expression of worship we can offer.[32] Thus, after giving ample space to

---

28. Waltke et al., *Psalms as Christian Lament*, 14.

29. Waltke et al., *Psalms as Christian Lament*, 15.

30. Gerald W. Peterman, "Longing to Lament," in Peterman and Schmutzer, *Between Pain and Grace*, 103–30.

31. Gerald W. Peterman, "Longing to Lament," in Peterman and Schmutzer, *Between Pain and Grace*, 103–30.

32. Card, *Sacred Sorrow*, 63. Theologian Don Saliers supports Card's claim that the most authentic worship results from suffering: "Christian public prayer finds praise and thanksgiving far less demanding when lamenting is suppressed . . . [and] praise and thanksgiving grow empty when the truth

express our own suffering, and for us to share the suffering of others, we must be corporately led in a remembrance of God's past acts of deliverance, either through the words of Scripture (the Psalms, Epistles, etc.) or new words by the congregation itself.[33] Modeling the psalmists, we are reminded of God's faithful acts of deliverance, and in the act of remembering are able to offer faith-filled, authentic praise, even in the presence of suffering.[34] The volatile nature of the world demands that church be a place of respite and a safe space for the honest, heartfelt expressions of suffering.

REGULAR RECITAL OF THE SHARED HISTORY OF BELIEVERS

A recurring central theme in the psalms of lament is the element of community. This theme is especially important in Psalms when the psalmist mourns the severing of community due to suffering. Psalm 22, for example, concludes with the sufferer rejoicing upon his return to community (vv. 22–23) and finally calling for others to join him in praise of Yahweh (v. 23). The element of community cannot be excluded if the suffering among us are to be holistically restored; the body of believers is integral during the time of suffering. The building of community through shared story and recitation of common history can maintain the healthy bonds needed when suffering strikes the individual. The recitation of God's deliverance of Israel was common, as found in Pss 78, 105, 106, and 136. Within each of these psalms are references to the sins of the people, the suffering of the nation, God's acts of deliverance, and the record of God's blessings to remind the people of God's mercy, faithfulness, and steadfast love.

The reiteration of this shared story of God's work on behalf of his people, according to Lee Roy Martin, "build[s] community

---

about human rage over suffering and injustice is never uttered. The revelatory character of prayer, liturgical or devotional, is diminished when no laments are ever raised." Saliers, *Worship as Theology*, 121.

33. Witvliet, *Biblical Psalms in Christian Worship*, 32.

34. Witvliet, *Biblical Psalms in Christian Worship*, 32.

and transmits the ethos of the community to new members and to the next generation."[35] In addition to connecting current and future generations, the shared story of God's delivering acts reminds us of our solidarity with generations past, and even the psalmists themselves. The shared story must hold suffering and rejoicing in tension, along with the common thread of God's faithful presence and the promise of Christ's coming kingdom. Thus, Martin states, instead of "a weekly convention of strangers," corporate worship is to be filled with people from all walks of life, broken and whole, sharing in the bearing of burdens, fulfilling Paul's command to "rejoice with those who rejoice, weep with those who weep" (Rom 12:15 NRSV).[36] The prayerful, sensitive selection of hymns, songs, and scriptural readings, with regular repetition, can begin to build the foundation upon which this shared story is built.

CONCLUSION

The rich gift of the psalms given to us has been an integral part of corporate worship beginning with their use in ancient Israel. The psalmists were ordinary people, dedicated to the service of God, who penned deeply expressive songs of individual and corporate worship. While separated from the psalmists by centuries of time, today we are still intimately connected to them by the covenant with Yahweh, by the element of shared humanity, and the broad range of emotions which result from daily living. Central to the psalmists was their connection in the heritage of those who lived under Yahweh's reign. Today we must remember that we, too, are a part of that heritage, and can thus borrow the words of the psalmists as we connect ourselves to this long line of worshipers.

Undergirding the cry of the psalmists for the church is the indescribable gift of Christ's redemptive suffering and resurrection, a gift over which the body of Christ can and should rejoice.

35. Lee Roy Martin, "The Book of Psalms and Pentecostal Worship," in Martin, *Toward a Pentecostal Theology*, 47–88.

36. Lee Roy Martin, "The Book of Psalms and Pentecostal Worship," in Martin, *Toward and Pentecostal Theology*, 47–88.

And yet, even with this life-altering reality, we continue to suffer in the post-9/11 world filled with wars, tragic loss, sickness, sin, and death. It is in the midst of this suffering that we can reach back and join in the psalmist's cries, even while reaching forward to the promise of Christ's coming kingdom, where John's prophecy of Rev 21:3–5 (NRSV) will be realized:

> And I heard a loud voice from the throne saying, "See, the home of God is among mortals. He will dwell with them; they will be his peoples, and God himself will be with them. He will wipe away every tear from their eyes, Death will be no more; mourning and crying and pain will be no more, for the first things have passed away."

In the face of suffering, within the tension held between pain and hope, the task of the worship leader is immense. Corporate song provides an environment where expressions of sorrow and wrestling with unanswered questions can be done safely, in community, as we share not only in the sorrow of one another in the local church but hear and uplift the cry of suffering and persecuted believers worldwide. The biblical precedent for such practices is undeniable. As the world becomes increasingly broken and sinful, we can draw upon the rich scriptural expressions found in the Psalms and throughout the canon, holding suffering and hope in tension until the unfolding of Christ's kingdom when tears will be no more.

6

The Fruits of Lament

We live in a time and place where over and over, when confronted with something unpleasant we pursue not coping but overcoming. Often we succeed.[1]

—Nicholas Wolterstorff

Though Scripture is filled with examples of people who cried out to God in their suffering, not least of whom was Jesus, Christians can still find it difficult to imagine why they should engage in the practice today. Didn't Jesus conquer death when he rose from the grave? Aren't we healed by his bruises? Our focus on the triumphalism of Christ has led us to adopt the idea that the predominant message of corporate worship should be one of victory and strength. A cursory study of modern worship music reveals a canon of songs filled with promises of victory, happiness, healing, and abundance. The cries of "How long, O Lord?" and "Hear my voice, O God" are far removed from anything we might sing or

1. Wolterstorff, *Lament for a Son*, 72.

even preach on any given Sunday. Celebration and praise have become the way we cope with pain, pushing it down, or even denying it because we fear acknowledging it might make God or our faith appear weak. While celebration and praise are certainly biblically mandated as part of gathered worship, they cannot become a tool by which we avoid engagement with the suffering around us.

Perhaps, then, it is important to consider what is lost when lament is excluded from corporate and private worship. Just as relationships between friends or in families are deepened and strengthened by endurance through hardships, so is the body of Christ built up and nourished when it engages in practices of lament during seasons of hardship. Don Saliers writes:

> Christian public prayer finds praise and thanksgiving far less demanding when lamenting is suppressed. Put differently, praise and thanksgiving grow empty when the truth about human rage over suffering and injustice is never uttered. Prayer may be sincere and God may certainly be praised and glorified in the absence of acknowledging such a truth about human suffering, but the revelatory character of prayer, liturgical or devotional, is diminished when no laments are ever raised.[2]

When lament is avoided, so too is the ability to confront and deal with suffering in all its forms. Author John Swinton writes about the car bomb detonated in Northern Ireland on a Saturday in August 1998 that killed 28 and injured 220. Awash in grief, Swinton longed to gather at his church with believers to mourn this tragedy. Throughout the entire church service the next day there was no mention of the bombing, no words of comfort spoken. Swinton writes:

> We had much space for love, joy, praise, and supplication, but it seemed that we viewed the acknowledgement of sadness and the tragic brokenness of our world as almost tantamount to faithlessness. As a result, when tragedy hit . . . we had no idea what to do with it or how to formulate our concerns. Because we had not consistently

2. Saliers, *Worship as Theology*, 121.

practiced the art of recognizing, accepting, and expressing sadness, we had not developed the capacity to deal
with tragedy. In the wake of the tragedy of Omagh, our
failure to publicly and communally acknowledge such a
major act of evil within our liturgical space demonstrated
our implicit tendency towards denial and avoidance.[3]

Lament is hard work. It demands something of us, forces us
to confront the darkness within ourselves and between us. Walking through hardships with those we love is not easy, and often
demands of us time and attention we would rather not give; so,
too, with lament in the body of Christ. Just as relationships are
strengthened by walking together through times of hardship, so
is the body of Christ as it ministers to one another and the world.

But do we lament merely for the sake of expressing difficult
emotions? What can we expect of ourselves and our community
when we implement lament? When we gather together for worship, we come not only to glorify and honor God, but also to grow
together in love, building up and edifying one another (Eph 4:16).
We are to suffer and rejoice together (1 Cor 12:27–31). The out-
comes of this fellowship can be seen as a kind of "fruit" or outcome
of the work of the liturgy. While the fruits of lament in the body of
Christ are many and varied, I will examine three: a greater intimacy with God and others, a vast compassion, and a genuine hope.

LAMENT ENABLES INTIMACY
WITH GOD AND OTHERS

In his book *Together: The Healing Power of Human Connection in
a Sometimes Lonely World*, United States Surgeon General Vivek
Murthy writes about the epidemic of loneliness he encountered as
he worked in 2014 to shape his health care agenda for the country.
Murthy sent his team out on a listening tour, asking one simple
question, "How can we help?"[4] While the team expected to hear

3. Swinton, *Raging with Compassion*, 92–93.
4. Murthy, *Together*, xiv.

concerns over the opioid epidemic or obesity, diabetes, and heart disease, one unexpected topic consistently rose to the surface: loneliness. Murthy noted, "It wasn't even identified directly as a health ailment. Loneliness ran like a dark thread through many of the more obvious issues that people brought to my attention, like addiction, violence, anxiety, and depression."[5] Murthy and his team interviewed families and individuals who repeatedly stated that one of the most difficult parts of their suffering was "at the hour of greatest need, they found themselves without the people they'd counted on for years."[6]

While Murthy heard story after story of deep-seated loneliness, he also heard stories around the power of community. One group of Native American teens shared with him how they "felt lost in their identity and forgotten by the outside world," and how they had started a program called "I Am Indian" to "strengthen a sense of culture and belonging among their peers and reduce their risk of alcohol and drug addiction."[7] Murthy came to understand that "while loneliness engenders despair and ever more isolation, togetherness raises optimism and creativity. When people feel they belong to one another, their lives are stronger, richer, and more joyful."[8]

Throughout his book, Murthy is careful to emphasize that loneliness is not just a sense of isolation, but "the subjective feeling that you're lacking the social connections you need . . . What's missing when you're lonely is the feeling of closeness, trust, and the affection of genuine friends, loved ones, and community."[9] Equally as crippling is the stigma, shame, and fear people feel that make loneliness a vicious cycle. Murthy writes:

> Because people tend to hide and deny their loneliness, others who might help . . . shy away from probing what seems like a sensitive emotional issue. Then the risk of self-destructive behaviors increases . . . In this way, the

5. Murthy, *Together*, xv.
6. Murthy, *Together*, xv.
7. Murthy, *Together*, xvi.
8. Murthy, *Together*, xvii.
9. Murthy, *Together*, 8.

combination of loneliness and stigma creates a cascade of consequences that affect not only our personal health and productivity, but also the health of society.[10]

Murthy writes that this cycle can be cut short by recognition and early intervention. Just as we recognize hunger and thirst as a signal to eat and drink, so too can we recognize loneliness as a signal to acknowledge our need for human connection.[11] The key is that such behavior must be learned.

British historian Fay Bound Alberti also makes the important distinction between being alone and being lonely. "Loneliness is not the state of being alone, then, though it is often mistaken as such. It is a conscious, cognitive feeling of estrangement or social separation from meaningful others; an emotional lack that concerns a person's place in the world."[12] Alberti also points to the shame inherent in loneliness, noting, "the interventions recommended tend to include increased contact with other people, without necessarily considering the difference between social contact and *meaningful* social contact, or the limitations that can be placed upon someone who wants to interact with others but is unable to due to health challenges, or personality traits like shyness."[13]

Other researchers like John Cacioppo write about the "subjective *experience* known as loneliness" rather than being physically alone.[14] Harvard history professor Jill Lepore writes about the parallels between loneliness and homelessness:

> Maybe what people experiencing loneliness and people experiencing homelessness both need are homes with other humans who love them and need them, and to know they are needed by them in societies that care about them. That's not a policy agenda. That's an indictment of modern life.[15]

10. Murthy, *Together*, 11.

11. Murthy, *Together*, 11.

12. Alberti, *Biography of Loneliness*, 5.

13. Alberti, *Biography of Loneliness*, 6, emphasis original.

14. Cacioppo, *Loneliness*, 5.

15. Lepore, "History of Loneliness," para. 7.

Perhaps this is an indictment of the church?

In Matt 25:34—40 (NRSV), Jesus' listeners are admonished to feed the hungry, welcome the stranger, clothe the naked, care for the sick, and visit the prisoners because "Truly I tell you, just as you did it to one of the least of these who are members of my family, you did it to me." Jesus' words echo those of the prophets who said, "Learn to do good; seek justice, rescue the oppressed, defend the orphan, plead for the widow" (Isa 1:17 NRSV). Or "He has told you, O mortal, what is good; and what does the LORD require of you but to do justice, and to love kindness, and to walk humbly with your God?" (Mic 6:8 NRSV). This is not merely an argument for social justice, but a call to carry out part of the very mission of Christ. It is an echo of Christ's description of his mission in Luke 4:18 (NRSV), "The Spirit of the Lord is upon me, because he has anointed me to bring good news to the poor. He has sent me to proclaim release to the captives and recovery of sight to the blind, to let the oppressed go free, to proclaim the year of the Lord's favor."

Lament can facilitate the opening of our hearts to the needs within ourselves and our families, our small groups and congregations, and in the world. When we share a service of lament over the loss of a church member, a tragedy in the community, or wars or natural disasters in our world that affect others, we sensitize our hearts to the very things that touched the heart of Christ and moved him with compassion. When we come together as one body, we join with the psalmists who chose to dialogue with God and lean into his promise to be "merciful and gracious, slow to anger, and abounding in steadfast love and faithfulness" (Exod 34:6 NRSV).

Services of lament can seem awkward at first, but as we build such a practice, we teach ourselves and our community "it is safe here," and our sorrows are welcomed and held not only by God, but by the body of Christ. Not every season of life is burdened down with sorrow, loneliness, and loss, but when periods of disorientation come, the tools we gain and the skills we learn from songs and sermons of lament will enable us to sit patiently with those who suffer, to bear the pain of the world in our own hearts and lift it up to God.

LAMENT ENABLES US TO BE WHO GOD IS

It is important, then, to examine our hearts and to cultivate patient awareness around our own suffering and that of others. Every time the church gathers for worship, there are deeply traumatic events taking place in individual lives, families, communities, and the world. Given this reality, it is important to ask how our liturgies are either ignoring or recognizing and leaning into the suffering. Do the songs we sing, the prayers we pray, the scriptures we read, and the sermons we preach hurry through or even ignore the hard work of lamenting trauma in favor of the ease of rejoicing? Are our practices cultivating a patient attentiveness that gives way to the kind of compassion modeled by Jesus?

The ministry of Jesus is defined by the compassion he showed to the suffering. While compassion is sometimes defined as taking pity or showing concern for the burdens of others, Jesus' brand of compassion was different because he removed the gap between himself and those who suffered, literally becoming like them. In doing so, Jesus modeled the difference between pity and compassion. While pity often functions to assuage the guilt of the helper, compassion "means that I identify with the afflicted individual so fully that I feed him for the same reason I feed myself: because we are both hungry."[16] Gregory Boyle describes how Jesus modeled this distinction,

> Jesus was not a man *for* others. He was one *with* others. There is a world of difference in that. Jesus didn't seek the rights of lepers. He *touched* the leper even before he got around to curing him. He didn't champion the cause of the outcast. He *was* the outcast. He didn't fight for improved conditions for the prisoner. He simply said, "I was in prison."[17]

In his suffering, Jesus broke the spiritual and physical barriers between himself and those to whom he ministered. Jesus did not walk amongst humankind as an untouchable "other," far removed

16. Zaretsky, *Subversive Simone Weil*, 46.

17. Boyle, *Tattoos on the Heart*, 72.

from humankind, unable to identify with their pain. Instead, as Phil 2:8 (NRSV) reminds us, he became like us, and "humbled himself by becoming obedient to the point of death—even death on a cross."

Despite this example set by Jesus, many things prevent Christians from living out the compassionate way of Jesus. In their book *Slow Church: Cultivating Community in the Patient Way of Jesus,* Christopher Smith and John Pattison point to a fundamental lack of patience deeply imbedded in culture that has also infiltrated the way we approach corporate worship, and especially the way we think about expressions of suffering.[18] Embedded in the very nature of suffering is an ambiguity that renders us incapable of knowing when the darkness will cease and we will once again step into the light. Our inability to wait, and our unwillingness to sing, preach, or pray uncomfortable words of lament often cuts us off from healing that can only come when suffering is voiced in a safe community.

By cultivating patience and a willingness to sit with the lonely and wounded, and bear witness to their suffering, we come to understand the true meaning of compassion. In short, we get to be like Christ. While pity seeks to provide a temporary solution, compassion calls us to commit to a long-term relationship of support born of the acknowledgement of our own suffering and fallibility. Tish Harrison Warren reminds us, "Jesus calls people to a cross—to die, to lose their life that they might gain it . . . he drank his own poison. He was honest about the cost of discipleship and about pain that is not easily solved."[19] Because of his own suffering, Jesus was able to model the empathetic essence of compassion. As Boyle states, "Compassion is not a relationship between the healer and the wounded. It's a covenant between equals . . . If we long to be in the world who God is, then, somehow our compassion has to find its way to vastness."[20] We feed the hungry, tend the sick, shelter the homeless, sit with the solitary because we, too, have known hunger, sickness, homelessness, and loneliness, because we, too, have suffered.

18. Smith and Pattison, *Slow Church*, 83.
19. Harrison Warren, *Prayer in the Night*, 144.
20. Boyle, *Tatoos on the Heart*, 66, 72.

LAMENT FOSTERS GENUINE HOPE

The practice of lament turns our eyes outward towards greater intimacy with and empathy for the suffering of others. This outward turn fosters compassion that enables us to come alongside those who suffer in empathy and be who God is in the world. Compassion then can foster within us an acknowledgement of the present brokenness held in tension with hope that looks forward to a time when all things will be made new, when every tear will be wiped away.

The New Testament writers wrote to a church enduring persecution. Rebekuh Eklund notes, "Nobody needs to be told to endure if things are going great."[21] And yet repeatedly we find reminders such as Paul's admonition to believers in 1 Cor 15:12–20 (NRSV) regarding the hope that outstrips any aspirations for happiness or fulfillment in the present,

> Now if Christ is preached as raised from the dead, how can some of you say that there is no resurrection of the dead? But if there is no resurrection of the dead, then Christ has not been raised; if Christ has not been raised, then our preaching is in vain and your faith is in vain. We are even found to be misrepresenting God, because we testified of God that he raised Christ, whom he did not raise if it is true that the dead are not raised. For if the dead are not raised, then Christ has not been raised. If Christ has not been raised, your faith is futile and you are still in your sins. Then those also who have fallen asleep in Christ have perished. If for this life only we have hoped in Christ, we are of all men most to be pitied.

Eugene Peterson translates verses 19–20 in *The Message*, "If all we get out of Christ is a little inspiration for a few short years, we're a pretty sorry lot. But the truth is that Christ *has* been raised up, the first in a long legacy of those who are going to leave the cemeteries." Later, this theme is picked up in 1 Peter 1:3 (NRSV), "He has given us new birth into a living hope through the resurrection of Jesus Christ from the dead, and to an inheritance which

21. Eklund, *Practicing Lament*, 41.

is imperishable, undefiled, and unfading, kept in heaven for you." This hope is "not based on scientific advance or social progress but on God himself. And this is not simply an intellectual belief but, as Peter says, it is a 'living hope.'"[22] Here, Timothy Keller emphasizes that Christian hope is not rooted in our own efforts to save ourselves, but purely and solely in what *Christ has done,* in *Christ's* resurrection. Grounding our suffering in this living hope compels us to place our confidence somewhere other than in our own efforts.

Genuine hope, therefore, calls us away from the here and now, away from the pursuit of a settled satisfaction gained through possessions or positions, breaking the endless loop of working, pushing, and striving to escape from or numb ourselves. Instead, hope born of lament calls us to sit in the tension between the present suffering and the promise of new life. Paul captures this tension in Rom 8:18–23 (NRSV),

> I consider that the sufferings of this present time are not worth comparing with the glory about to be revealed to us. For the creation waits with eager longing for the revealing of the children of God; for the creation was subjected to futility not of its own will but by the will of the one who subjected it, in hope that the creation itself will be set free from its bondage to decay and will obtain the freedom of the glory of the children of God. We know that the whole creation has been groaning in labor pains until now; and not only the creation but we ourselves, who have the first fruits of the Spirit, groan inwardly while we wait for adoption, the redemption of our bodies.

C. Clifton Black compares Paul's metaphor of birth to Jeremiah's sorrow over Jerusalem in Lamentations. Jeremiah is sitting in the rubble of a once bustling city, grieving for the lost glory when a memory of God's promise of steadfast love resurfaces in Lamentations 3:22 (NRSV), "The steadfast love of the LORD never ceases, his mercies never come to an end; they are new every morning;

22. Keller, *Hope in Times of Fear*, xx.

great is your faithfulness. 'The LORD is my portion,' says my soul, 'therefore I will hope in him.'" Black comments,

> Poet and apostle bear witness to the corporate dimension of lament. A metropolis is laid waste. A survivor stumbles through smoldering rubble, offering an elegy for Jerusalem. Centuries later, on this side of Easter, Paul invites the church to Rome to wait with him in a birthing room. It is the cosmos, God's creation in its entirety, that writhes in travail, beginning to give birth to a glory only glimpsed and to this day not yet fully delivered. Like the poet and the apostle, we are not detached spectators. We too are seized by besetting, universal pangs: the ache— subsiding only long enough to redouble its inexpressible intensity—that empties all memory of happiness.
>
> Yet the spine of lament is hope: not the vacuous optimism that "things will get better," which in the short run is usually a lie. But the deep irrepressible conviction, in the teeth of present evidence, that God has not severed the umbilical cord that has always bound us to the Lord.[23]

Hope, then, is not positive thinking, nor is it optimism. Hope is a *remembrance*. It is a reminder of "Emmanuel, which means 'God with us'" (Matt 1:23 NRSV), and El Shaddai, "God Almighty" (Gen 17:1 NRSV). It is a reminder of both the victorious *and* the suffering Christ.

If our corporate practices of singing, preaching, and praying only contain assurances of triumph and victory as though being a Christian precludes suffering, then our liturgical practices are misaligned with Scripture. Instead, by balancing lament with praise, we avoid conflating faith with positive thinking and the "self-deceptive refusal to acknowledge things for how they really are."[24] In so doing, lament becomes the seedbed for hope and praise by allowing us to name our feelings in the presence of God and other believers. In naming our feelings we create space in which

23. C. Clifton Black, "The Persistence of the Wounds," in Brown and Miller, *Lament*, 47–58.

24. Nancy J. Duff, "Recovering Lamentation as a Practice in the Church," in Brown and Miller, *Lament*, 3–14

to process feelings, to understand the nature of long-suffering, and thus know we are not alone on our journey.

THE FORMATIVE POWER OF LAMENT

The fruits of lament—greater intimacy with God and others, vast compassion in the way of Christ, and the fostering of genuine hope—are born of times of intentional, patient expressions of sorrow in the presence of God and others. They expand our view of God, and help to align us with the mission of Christ to the world.

In his deeply moving response after the death of his son, Eric, in a rock-climbing accident, Nicholas Wolterstorff admits that, even after suffering such a soul crushing loss,

> I still don't fully know what it's like to be one of those mothers one sees in poverty posters, soup tin in hand, bloated child alongside, utterly dependent for her very existence on the largesse of others. I still don't fully know what it's like to be a member of a people whose whole national existence is under attack, Armenian or Jew or Palestinian. Yet I now know more of it.[25]

And this is, perhaps, the central outcome of lament—that we would know more of the suffering of others. Is this not why Jesus came? So that we would know we "do not have a high priest who is unable to sympathize with our weaknesses"? (Heb 4:15 NRSV). "Suffering both bonds and differentiates us," write Kathleen Billman and Daniel Migliore.[26] And while our ways of suffering may be uniquely individualized, by sharing our suffering in times of lament, "we may become deeply aware of a common vulnerability and anguish—a sense of shared *humanity*—that helps us place our suffering in a larger context and experience a new sense of connection with other suffering human beings amidst our own pain."[27]

---

25. Wolterstorff, *Lament for a Son*, 72.

26. Billman and Migliore, *Rachel's Cry*, 123.

27. Billman and Migliore, *Rachel's Cry*, 123, emphasis original.

These are the fruits of lament that demonstrate the formative power of suffering done in community. John Swinton reminds us, "If our liturgical practices do not take onboard the full breadth of human experiences, our formation will be incomplete."[28] Lament is the hallway that leads to hope and rejoicing. Lament in worship calls us to turn our hearts outward to the suffering of the world, to the suffering near to the heart of God. Our formation, then, is more and more complete, bound up in the love of Christ for the world.

28. Swinton, *Finding Jesus in the Storm*, 208.

7

Worship Case Studies and Recommendations for Further Research

IN RECENT YEARS, USE of the Psalms in Christian worship has been on the rise and has included the use of the laments. Among the catalysts for this renewal have been new books and recordings whose creators birthed them after seasons of struggle, often times of personal loss or loss in the lives of loved ones. Recent notable examples of such creative work have been produced by artists and scholars who having endured either a painful event or a prolonged period of suffering, have found in the psalms of lament a rich resource that is both cathartic and healing. Such expressions, therefore, are often only birthed after a period of personal or communal tragedy.

WORSHIP CASE STUDIES

Four case studies of recent musical or scholarly projects will be discussed that demonstrate ways in which lament psalms have become a means of expression to pray through and process experiences of suffering or tragedy: (1) recording by Sandra McCracken of select psalms, with particular focus on her use of Ps 42 and the healing it brought during a period of personal suffering;[1] (2) the scholarly study of the Psalms by Ray Van Neste and C. Richard Wells birthed out of the aftermath of a tornado that struck Union University in 2008;[2] (3) the multiple layers of suffering in the life and ministry of Michael Card which resulted in pastoral and devotional literature and songs on the subject of lament;[3] and (4) the work of American Slater Armstrong whose compassion for suffering Christians in Sudan, Africa, resulted in a recording of original songs using indigenous instrumentation and the voices of the Sudanese people to express both hope and joy in the presence of unprecedented and protracted suffering.[4] The chapter concludes with an examination of parallel studies that intersect and resonate with corporate lament expressions, and suggested areas for further study.

SANDRA MCCRACKEN: PERSONAL USE OF THE LAMENT PSALMS

Sandra McCracken is a song and hymn writer whose 2015 recording *Psalms* was in great part an expression of her personal sorrow during a period of deep suffering.[5] In a 2015 interview with The Gospel Coalition in which she referenced her suffering, McCracken described the psalms as "invitational," in the sense that they invite believers into intimacy with God. McCracken commented,

> The Psalms are by nature invitational. I recently asked a pastor-friend about how he would describe healthy relational intimacy, asking what it looks like within marriage or within close community. He said that the first word he thinks of that displays intimacy between two people is *invitation*. When God included the poetry of the Psalms

1. McCracken, *Psalms*.
2. Wells and Van Neste, *Forgotten Songs*.
3. Card, *Sacred Sorrow*.
4. Armstrong, *Even in Sorrow*.
5. McCracken, *Psalms*.

in his letter to us, he made a move toward us that invites us more deeply toward him, with our affections and with our emotion.[6]

McCracken continued in the interview, emphasizing how believers who are caught up in the daily task of living rarely have time to reflect on deeper feelings and emotions and how these are evidenced in interactions and behaviors.[7] According to McCracken, "Often it takes a painful life-disruption before we stop and reflect on what's beneath the surface of the life we have built."[8] Although the psalms were part of her daily devotional practice, McCracken admits that the inspiration to versify and set these texts to music came out of her own time of suffering.[9]

On her album McCracken includes three versifications of lament psalms: 42 ("My Help, My God"), 43 ("Send Out Your light"), and 62 ("My Soul Finds Rest").[10] A fourth song includes the cry, "O LORD, have mercy," found in many of the laments, including Psalms 25, 51, and 123. According to McCracken, the song "My Help, My God," a versification of Ps 42 (NRSV), became a repeated and beloved anthem during the most difficult period of her suffering.[11] This Psalm concludes with the psalmist encouraging himself: "Why are you cast down, O my soul, and why are you disquieted within me? Hope in God; for I shall again praise him, my help and my God." This verse is also found in Psalm 43 and is included in the song "Send Out Your Light."[12]

As a result of her journey through sorrow and lament, McCracken concludes that the psalms are a source of expression when a believer's own ability to verbally express their pain is silenced as they enable one to "go deeper into honest sorrow," because "we

6. Mesa, "Sandra McCracken on Life, Loss, and Longing."
7. Mesa, "Sandra McCracken on Life, Loss, and Longing."
8. Mesa, "Sandra McCracken on Life, Loss, and Longing."
9. McCracken, "Songs of Praise, Lament, and Hope."
10. McCracken, *Psalms*.
11. McCracken, "My Help, My God."
12. McCracken, "Send Out Your Light."

are not the first to feel what we feel."[13] While some of McCracken's psalm versifications are individual prayers, she states that she has been recently burdened to write versions more appropriate for congregational use.[14] While acknowledging that the present culture avoids personal expressions of grief in favor of success and triumphalism, McCracken believes the church must "fight against the dishonesty of living on the surface of things, or encouraging people to put a smile on their faces so they will have a positive attitude about difficult things."[15]

McCracken's journey into and through a period of suffering resulted in a change in mood of her performances from extroverted and lighthearted to more contemplative and introspective expressions. While she acknowledges in the interview that in the future her journey may turn back to a period where every performance is a "party," at present the sorrow has led her to use the psalmic laments as a new and different lens through which to view and process life.[16] Her long season of growth has birthed a new set of devotional resources for the layperson and a desire in McCracken herself to write and produce laments for congregational use.

In her embrace and reworking of the psalms, in this project McCracken is an example of someone accessing these ancient songs in order to express and pray specific emotions, and particularly those of sorrow. In doing so, she taught others to align themselves with the emotions of the psalmists. This type of personal/devotional use of the Psalms can aid in restoring believers to the community of faith, while at the same time enriching the dialogical relationship with God so deeply valued by the psalmists themselves.

13. Mesa, "Sandra McCracken on Life, Loss, and Longing."
14. McCracken, "Songs of Praise, Lament, and Hope."
15. Mesa, "Sandra McCracken on Life, Loss, and Longing."
16. "Conversation with Singer-Songwriter Sandra McCracken."

C. RICHARD WELLS AND RAY VAN NESTE: THE LAMENT PSALMS IN COMMUNITY

The beauty of the psalms is in part due to their versatility, in that they can function in virtually every setting of the church's ministry, from personal use and scholarly study to pastoral care. Ray Van Neste and C. Richard Wells, both members of the faculty at Union University, compiled the book *Forgotten Songs: Reclaiming the Psalms for Christian Worship*, from papers given during a conference on the Psalms at their institution in 2008.[17] Earlier that year, just prior to the originally scheduled conference date of February 2008, the university was struck by a massive tornado that destroyed a large part of the campus. Covering a span of topics, the chapters explore how the psalms serve as a guide for Christian life and worship, both in times of joy and pain. In the preface to the book, Van Neste shares how he and his colleague, professor of music Dr. Betty Bedsole, settled on the Psalms precisely because of the devastating circumstances through which their university community had come. Although the suffering and massive loss experienced was communal rather than personal, the authors' foundational reason for turning to the Psalms was much the same as McCracken's: they found in the Psalter a means for processing and expressing emotion, prayer, and healing from immense tragedy.

Van Neste elaborates on the purpose and foundation for the study in the preface of the book, noting that at previous points in the history of the church, the psalms were a consistent source of inspiration and reformation for this process.[18] Using this historic foundation, Van Neste and Wells divided the book into two sections: (1) biblical and historical foundations for use of the psalms, which explores how the psalms are formative for corporate practices of prayer, not only in the early church, but also in ancient Israel and in the worship practices of Christ and his disciples, and (2) incorporating the psalms into modern worship practices, which offers practical examples of how to sing the psalms in corporate

17. Wells and Van Neste, *Forgotten Songs*, xiii.
18. Wells and Van Neste, *Forgotten Songs*, 2.

worship, including the lament psalms. The book concludes with an annotated bibliography of resources for those desiring to implement the Psalms into corporate worship.

Birthed out of tragedy, this collection of essays covers a spectrum of ways—from scholarly work to practical ministry application—for incorporating Psalms into the life of the church. It is a resource that brings with it a depth of insight from the community's journey through suffering in the voices of various authors, including faculty, staff, and students within the Union University community. The book demonstrates the ways in which suffering and lament are able to create out of pain an offering that can serve and minister to the community of believers, and help to refine and mature, even transform their worldview by evoking deep gratitude and a greater pursuit of relationship with God and one another.

MICHAEL CARD: PASTORAL AND DEVOTIONAL USE OF THE LAMENT PSALMS

Singer-songwriter and author Michael Card has for several years directed the focus of his artistic efforts to restoring lament in the devotional life and pastoral literature of the church. In his book *A Sacred Sorrow: Reaching Out to God in the Lost Language of Lament*, Card shares the story of a postcard he received from theologian and scholar Calvin Seerveld shortly after the terrorist attacks of September 11, 2001, that read, "See, you have no songs to sing."[19] Seerveld's terse note inspired Card to compose laments and to equip others to do the same. It was also the final catalyst for Card's watershed book that brought suffering to the forefront of evangelical Christian consciousness—at least for those who had ears to hear, and inspired the production of his subsequent recording, *The Hidden Face of God*, hymns and original songs of lament.[20]

Prior to the events of 9/11, Card shares in the book he had faced tragedy and profound loss in his personal life and the lives of

19. Card, *Sacred Sorrow*, 7; Card, "General Session 6, part 1."
20. Card, *Hidden Face of God*.

close family members. In the space of thirteen months, his sister had lost two unborn children, and his son was arrested on three different occasions.[21] Card relates how the long season of sorrow over his son's self-destructive lifestyle brought to him a greater understanding of God's *hesed*, the Hebrew word which permeates the Psalms often translated as God's "lovingkindness," a concept which Card explains as the essence of the gospel.[22] The pain of his son's arrests and other tragic events in Card's personal journey reached a personal climax for him following the attacks on the nation on 9/11, driving the direction of his entire ministry to the study, writing, and teaching of biblical lament from that time on.

As a result of his own journey, Card concluded that the rhythm of suffering followed by lament is part of the biblical model of the journey that every believer will experience.[23] This journey is not only modeled in the life of key biblical figures (i.e., Job), but also throughout the entirety of Scripture, which models the movement from knowing God as a "concept," to knowing him as a "person," and in "relationship."[24] Card's personal journey of suffering led him to conclude, therefore, that "all worship begins in the wilderness," and it is in the wilderness that one finds that the most precious gift one can offer to God is "the thing that hurts you most."[25] In the process of Card's working through these concepts and his own suffering over the years, he produced a series of books and songs, albums, and conference lectures that invite believers to share their sorrows with God, both individually and corporately, and enable them individually and corporately to move through the wilderness of lament into the rich relationship with God brought about as a result of the journey. Card's music serves as an example of the diversity of themes that can come from the Psalms and how they can be crafted for both individual and corporate use. His

21. Card, "General Session 6, part 1."
22. Card, *Sacred Sorrow*, 15.
23. Card, "General Session 6, part 1."
24. Card, "General Session 6, part 1."
25. Card, "General Session 6, part 1."

work demonstrates the multivalent nature of the psalms of lament for use in personal devotion as well as for pastoral care.

SUDAN, AFRICA: GLOBAL LAMENT TRADITIONS

Outside the North American context the need for lament resources is great due to widespread persecution of Christians in areas such as Sudan. In her article on the use of the arts in trauma healing, Harriet Hill, program director for the Trauma Healing Institute of The American Bible Society contends, "For traumatized people to find healing, they need to express their pain."[26] Hill notes that most African cultures adhere to a lament tradition that can incorporate melody, poetry, dance, or a specific posture.[27] Sadly, those unfamiliar with African cultures have at times labeled such traditions as "heathen" or "off-limits," according to Hill.[28] While these expressions may seem foreign to those outside the African context, when compared with the psalmic laments, such demonstrations are more in line with the biblical responses to suffering in ancient Israel than non-expressive Western modes of response to pain.[29]

A striking example of worship born out of suffering is captured on the recording by Slater Armstrong of Sudanese Christians who have suffered persecution and even death as a result of a civil war that lasted many decades in their country.[30] Armstrong, serving at the time as a worship leader in Louisiana, first heard the story of atrocities suffered by the Dinka community in the late 1990s, when many of their people were forced into slavery during

26. Harriet Hill, "The Arts and Trauma Healing," in Krabill, *Worship and Mission*, 175–79.

27. Harriet Hill, "The Arts and Trauma Healing" in Krabill, *Worship and Mission*, 175–79.

28. Harriet Hill, "The Arts and Trauma Healing," in Krabill, *Worship and Mission*, 175–79.

29. Harriet Hill, "The Arts and Trauma Healing," in Krabill, *Worship and Mission*, 175–79.

30. George Luke, "Eritrea and Sudan: Worship in the Midst of Suffering," in Krabill, *Worship and Mission*, 200–203. Armstrong, *Even in Sorrow*.

the war.[31] Armstrong travelled to Sudan in 1999, and recorded the singing of Dinka congregations and choirs of adults and children on the album entitled *Even in Sorrow: A Recorded Project for the Persecuted Church in Sudan*.[32] The album, which was released in 2002, also included some native instruments. Most of the songs feature amazingly up-tempo tune styles despite lyrics that express deep sorrow over the loss suffered by the people. The song "Children of God" details the terror of an enemy raid at night during which the Dinka believers were brutally beaten, sexually abused, and many captured and sent into slavery.[33] This song holds in tension the brutality of the suffering and the fact that the people are "children of God," calling on other Christians to realize their plight and offer help. The most closely psalm-based song on the album, "Praise Jehovah," expresses trust in God that is born of oppression and loss.[34] Reflecting a confidence and praise born of sorrow, the song echoes psalm passages such as 18:1–6, which reflect the confident speech of one who has experienced sorrow and whose cry was heard by God.

Armstrong's *Even in Sorrow* captures grippingly honest songs of both trust and sorrow being created amid suffering, persecution, and loss by Christians across the world. It is also a glimpse into the way in which cultures outside North America use their art forms to process suffering and bring it to speech. Armstrong's recording captures a body of congregational songs that may seem to many Westerners incongruously joyful and upbeat even though many of their lyrics clearly express the deep losses of the church in Sudan. The use of indigenous native instruments, including various African drums, allowed the people to bring their own unique identity even while expressing the universal cry of those who have been persecuted.

31. George Luke, "Eritrea and Sudan," in Krabill, *Worship and Mission*, 200–203.

32. Armstrong, *Even in Sorrow*.

33. Lyrics cited from Armstrong, "Children of God," track 3, *Even in Sorrow*.

34. Lyrics cited from Armstrong, "Praise Jehovah," track 5, *Even in Sorrow*.

PARALLEL STUDIES

The subject of corporate lament intersects with a range of related topics that have received recent scholarly attention from worship scholars, biblical scholars, theologians, musicians, and artists. These models have undertaken specific questions regarding worship practices, questions which influence and are influenced by corporate lament. Several representative example studies will be presented in this section in order to demonstrate this intersection and to encourage further exploration of other connecting studies.

David Duke: Typologies of Lament Hymns

In his article "Giving Voice to Suffering in Worship: A Study in the Theodicies of Hymnody," David Duke argues that hymns represent liturgy of non-liturgical traditions, and as such, shape and reflect the beliefs of the people.[35] Duke believes congregational song should allow believers to express lament as an integral part of the relationship with God, bringing the suffering into his presence.[36] In this comparative study of five hymns by both Isaac Watts and Anne Steele, Duke explores ways in which their respective hymns encourage or discourage worshipers to respond to their suffering, either individually or corporately. From this comparison, Duke develops a typology of lament hymns which includes:[37]

1. Hymns of *explanation*: give reasons for pain and function as theodicies; are impersonal and focus on the cognitive.[38]

2. Hymns of *assurance*: pastoral in tone, express Christian belief; remind believers of historical suffering of the saints and their endurance by God's grace.[39]

---

35. Duke, "Giving Voice to Suffering in Worship," 263.
36. Duke, "Giving Voice to Suffering in Worship," 263.
37. Duke, "Giving Voice to Suffering in Worship," 266–71.
38. Duke, "Giving Voice to Suffering in Worship," 266.
39. Duke, "Giving Voice to Suffering in Worship," 268.

3. Hymns of *Lament:* may include confession of trust; work to identify and name pain; appeal for God's help; often express frustration; question the care of the community and even God; recall and long for comfort of past life; can contain all or a portion of elements from the lament psalms (address, plea, complaint, petition, confession of trust).[40]

Duke's article presents a foundation upon which to build future studies of congregational song, and also a lens through which scholars may examine current worship song for its ability to adequately give expression to suffering believers.

Sibley Towner: Comparative Study— the Psalms and Modern Hymnals

Basing his study on the premise that the hymnal represents a "second canon of accepted teaching," and which although lacking the authority of Scripture, is nonetheless supportive of the theological teachings of the church, Sibley Towner has undertaken an examination of five hymnals published since 1985, focusing on hymns that present an entire biblical psalm or at least a large portion of a given psalm.[41] Towner begins by categorizing each hymn according to Hermann Gunkel's classification of the Psalms, including both individual and communal laments.[42] Towner's study reveals that the laments, both individual and communal, rank lowest in number of psalm types represented across all five hymnals, with only "prophetic oracles of judgment" ranking lower.[43] This imbalance of hymn types reveals a distinct deficiency in hymns that cover the range of emotions found in the Psalms. The hymnals

40. Duke, "Giving Voice to Suffering," 270.

41. Sibley Towner, "Without Our Aid He Did Us Make," in Strawn and Bowen, *A God So Near*, 17–34. Hymnals examined are *Psalter Hymnal*, 1987; *The United Methodist Hymnal*, 1989; *The Presbyterian Hymnal*, 1990; *Rejoice in the Lord*, 1985; and *The New Century Hymnal*, 1995.

42. Gunkel, *Psalms: A Form-Critical Introduction*, 1967.

43. Sibley Towner, "Without Our Aid He Did Us Make," in Strawn and Bowen, *A God So Near*, 17–34.

surveyed leaned heavily toward praise and thanksgiving themes which, though important, must be balanced with expressions of sorrow, he argues. Towner notes that congregations prefer to celebrate God as "creator" and "liberator," rather than "lament to the God who listens."[44] Given this imbalance, Towner concludes, "In the competitive denominational marketplace of the twenty-first century, somber doesn't sell. We prefer to sin and repent, lament and die in silent privacy."[45]

Towner's study of these five major recent North American hymnals is foundational for the study of corporate worship music as a whole. His study reveals that the rich presence of lament found in the Psalms is largely lacking in current Protestant North American congregational song, and that the repercussions of this absence are the breakdown in community which results in believers who suffer alone.

Matthew Westerholm: Inaugurated Eschatology in Congregational Song

In his study of contemporary American hymnody, Matthew Westerholm examines the most-used congregational worship music between 2000 and the end of 2015, with attention to how themes of inaugurated eschatology in corporate song influence spiritual formation and self-identity in US evangelical churches.[46] The goal of the study is to use lyrics of worship songs to ascertain how a congregation understands and accepts particular church doctrines, and the subsequent changes this might bring to how evangelicals understand and define themselves.[47] Westerholm's study reveals a sharp decline in the presence of themes of inaugurated eschatology ("already-and-not-yet"), especially that of the

44. Sibley Towner, "Without Our Aid He Did Us Make," in Strawn and Bowen, *A God So Near*, 17–34.

45. Sibley Towner, "Without Our Aid He Did Us Make," in Strawn and Bowen, *A God So Near*, 17–34.

46. Westerholm, "'Hour Is Coming and Is Now Here,'" 3.

47. Westerholm, "'Hour Is Coming and Is Now Here,'" 3.

"not-yet," in contemporary worship music, and offers suggestions on how these themes can be restored.

Westerholm's study is vital for a clear understanding and re-implementation of corporate lament practices in that it reminds believers of the dangers inherent in focusing on the "already," which leave little space for the cry of Rev 22:20 (NRSV), "Come, Lord Jesus!" The absence of eschatological themes can lead believers to seek solace in the present, and to lose a vital dimension of Christ's work on the cross which inaugurated the coming of his kingdom when suffering would cease. This loss, Westerholm argues, silences the church's voice of lament in favor of triumphalist and perfectionist expectations that lead believers to seek happiness and contentment in the "now," rather than groaning for the coming of Christ's kingdom (Rom 8:23).[48] Such a philosophy marginalizes believers who experience suffering, according to Westerholm:

> If worshipers had an exciting week, the "already" service affirms their experience. But if their week had more trial than triumph, they leave the service disappointed. When the leaders are not as perfect as they appear, worshipers (especially the young) leave the church devastated. . . . When evangelical worship services imply that believers should experience complete victory now, the church is creating expectations that it cannot meet; it is preparing its people for disappointment.[49]

The present study of lament confirms Westerholm's premise that congregational song must equip believers with balanced language which allows them to both praise God and to lament before him.

Westerholm's attention to themes of inaugurated eschatology in contemporary worship music is vital if the church is to provide space for its members to cry out to God in their personal suffering, for the suffering of the congregation or community as a whole, and for the persecuted church at large. If given permission and time to lament in a space that is safe and where believers may come

48. Westerholm, "'Hour Is Coming and Is Now Here,'" 178.
49. Westerholm, "'Hour Is Coming and Is Now Here,'" 178.

together to cry out as the psalmists did, a healthy church can be nurtured that longs and cries out for the return of Christ's kingdom when sorrow and tears will be no more.

Rebecca Messbarger and Philip Woodmore: Instilling the Psalms for Periods of Crisis

The COVID-19 pandemic which began in 2020 has resulted in the greatest loss of life across the world in many decades. In slightly over two years, more than six million people across the world have lost their lives to the deadly virus.[50] Compounding these losses is the fact that many of the victims were forced to die alone in hospital wards attended only by exhausted doctors, nurses, and medical staff, with no immediate family allowed due to the high transmissibility of the virus. It was a crisis the size of which few had ever experienced.

Rebecca Messbarger, Director of Medical Humanities at Washington University in St. Louis, Missouri, and Philip A. Woodmore, composer and music educator, recently joined to host an event in honor of those whose lives were lost and those left to grieve. Held on April 23, 2022, the event was hosted in Forest Park in St. Louis where attendees joined together in darkness near the park's Grand Basin which was surrounded by 1,500 paper lanterns lit in remembrance of those who had died. Participants heard remarks from local pastors, and joined together in song and prayer as memories were shared about those affected by loss.

Local Episcopal pastor and event speaker, Reverend Mike Angell, commented,

> The lack of a space for grief is one of the things that is a big loss in a pandemic. It means something to mark a life by coming together and saying ancient prayers and going through those motions, yes. But just showing up for one another in some ways is an important part of how we mark that life.[51]

50. "WHO Coronavirus (COVID-19) Dashboard."
51. Otten and Byard, "Requiem of Light."

"Grief is dark and it's often lonely," stated Messbarger.[52] Events such as these, therefore, serve as both an outlet for difficult emotions and a kind of structure around which we can shape and make sense of our pain in community. The loneliness of suffering is softened by the joining together of many people whose lives have been similarly affected. Philip Woodmore, whose piece "Our Story: Sharing the Voices We Have Lost from COVID-19" was performed during the event, commented,

> For me, "Requiem of Light" is a moment to pause. It is a moment of stillness, a moment of silence and reflection . . . We all experience that moment in different ways. Some will be sad, some will be angry, some will be joyous. You just never really know what that grief is going to look like until you go through it.[53]

Woodmore's reminder that all people experience grief differently also captures the multivalent applications of the Psalms, and especially of the laments.

Periods of widespread and protracted grief such as was experienced during the COVID-19 pandemic require authentic and unfiltered expressions such as those found in the psalms of lament. As these ancient prayers give expression to individual suffering, they in turn call us to turn our hearts outward to others across the world who have suffered similar loss, and "move us beyond sadness and into compassion."[54]

Interdisciplinary Use of the Psalms

The multivalent nature of the psalms makes them valuable in many areas of ministry and academic disciplines, including theology, worship and congregational song, and counseling and psychology. In a survey of articles on songs and hymns from the Bible, Chris Angel discusses recent studies by authors who have applied

52. Otten, "Requiem of Light in Forest Park April 23."
53. Otten and Byard, "Requiem of Light."
54. Otten and Byard, "Requiem of Light."

expertise from various fields to the study and use of the Psalms, as well as other hymnic passages found in Scripture.[55] Particularly relevant to the topic of corporate lament practices is the article by Daniel Estes, which examines the intertextual usage of Ps 78:1–8 throughout the canon, particularly in Deuteronomy and Proverbs.[56] Estes also examines the psalm as poetry and song, noting the effect of these artistic forms on the student, and the ways in which they enable the reader or singer to undergo and encounter feelings similar to that of the author.[57] Angel notes that Estes goes one step further and encourages the interdisciplinary study of the psalms from the viewpoint of cognitive psychology and neurology.[58]

Estes's work relates to that of psychiatrist Curt Thompson, who has conducted a similar study on the integration of neuroscience and spirituality, and who cites specific psalm passages that support this integration.[59] Due to the depth and breadth of emotional expressions they contain, the psalms, and particularly the laments, serve not only as tools for believers to pray and express the emotions of suffering, but also point to the need for new scholarship at the intersection of biblical and theological study, applied ministry, and neuroscience and psychology.

The Necessity of Lament in Preaching and Song

Luke Powery and Thomas G. Long have both produced recent work on the need for emotionally honest preaching based on biblical lament drawn from the Revelation and from the Psalms, respectively.[60] Powery examines the worship hymns found in Revelation 5:1–14, with special attention to the "countercultural portrayal" of the crucified Lamb who has suffered for mankind over against

55. Angel, "Sing a New Song," 33–34.
56. Estes, "Psalm 78:1–8 as a Musical Intertext," 34.
57. Angel, "Sing a New Song," 34.
58. Angel, "Sing a New Song," 34.
59. Thompson, *Anatomy of the Soul*, 163–71.
60. Powery, "Painful Praise," 69–78; Long, "Four Ways to Preach a Psalm," 21–32, 34.

the triumphalism of the Roman Empire.[61] His article focuses on the tension found in the Revelation hymn that expresses both rejoicing and suffering, and makes a plea for this same balance in both congregational song and preaching: "Singing and preaching hymns does not exclude the agony and tragedy of humanity but praises and preaches through, in, and against the cancerous pain of human life."[62] In a similar argument, Thomas Long calls for more preaching texts based on the Psalms in order to "[keep] their poetic power laced more firmly into the larger theological fabric of faith."[63]

The regular use of the Psalms in Christian preaching, teaching, and song equips believers with poetic expressions that can be integrated into the regular vocabulary of prayer, and in turn cultivates a rich atmosphere for soul care within the gathered church.

STUDIES NEEDED

This study of corporate lament sought to lay the biblical foundations for a theology of suffering and its application to ministry, specifically worship ministry, in the local church. This section will suggest representative studies that need to be undertaken in the area of corporate lament.

The Psalms and the Liturgical Calendar

The historic reading and singing of the entire Psalter throughout the church year and methods for its implementation in all denominational practices is an area in which ministry tools are needed. Methods and worship ministry guides for the implementation of the lament psalms in penitential seasons of Holy Week and Advent must be crafted to familiarize leaders with their rich and descriptive language so appropriate for these seasons. Such

---

61. Angel, "Sing a New Song," 34.
62. Powery, "Painful Praise," 77. See also: Powery, *Ways of the Word*.
63. Long, "Four Ways to Preach a Psalm," 23.

practices would require musicians capable of versifying the Psalms to create new paraphrases suitable for congregational use at specific liturgical seasons. These projects could start with the metrical psalms and melodies in the Genevan Psalter, as has been done by a group of musicians in The Psalms Project, led by Shane Heilman, a singer-songwriter, guitarist, and worship leader from Sioux Falls, South Dakota, and a group of professional musicians, worship leaders, and song writers.[64] A project of massive proportions is *Psalms Reborn*, by nationally-known sacred jazz musician Chuck Marohnic, who created new, original settings for the entire book of Psalms to music in a wide variety of genres and related musical idioms of jazz for solo, ensemble, and choir settings.[65]

Hymns of Lament for Specialized Services

The psalms can serve a key role for pastoral leaders and those trained in specialized soul care professions such as counseling, chaplaincy, and social work. The use of the lament psalms can play a central role in the bereavement process for professionals who lead individuals or groups through times of suffering and loss. Leading grief specialist, music therapist, and long-time hospice director, Joy Berger, wrote an important recent study that examines the central role of music to the grief process. Berger's work draws from theories and methods of music therapy, chaplaincy training, and her own past journey through devastating personal loss. An important study would examine how the psalms of lament could further enrich and enhance these theories and methods and enable the suffering to draw from these ancient words both for prayer and expression of pain.

There is a need for ministry tools detailing the use of the psalms, and particularly the laments, when ministering in a prison context. In this setting, expressions of grief over personal suffering may be mingled with themes of remorse over sin. There is a need

64. The Psalms Project, "Psalms 1–10," vol. 1; "Psalms 11–20," vol. 2; "Psalms 21–30."

65. Marohnic, "Psalms Reborn."

for psalms of pleading as well as those of assurance of God's faithful presence. Scholarly studies on the use of psalms in prison ministry could include interviews with current and former inmates or with chaplains or others who have served in this vital area of ministry.

Finally, psalm-based resources for prayer retreats, divorce recovery support groups, mental health support and recovery, and groups for the recently bereaved are needed. The psalms of lament could provide words to express suffering for those to whom words have been lost due to the depth of grief. Ministry tools on the use of psalms of lament with those actively dying and with their family members engaged in anticipatory grieving could be fruitful for equipping young or inexperienced pastors, as they comfort the grieving and facilitate expression of their sorrow.

Studies in Historical Periods of Congregational Song

Historical studies that trace the use of the lament psalms in Christian (specifically Protestant) worship traditions are needed as well. Every era of church history can be fruitfully examined from the perspective of how they have dealt with suffering and lament through an examination of the hymnody of the era. In evangelical worship particularly, such studies are needed to document the decline of lament, beginning with the urban revival of the era of the late nineteenth century through the present era of contemporary Christian worship music.

Methodologies for the study of hymns of these historical periods can include the comparison of lament themes drawn from the output of particular hymns writers, such as in the study by Duke previously referenced.[66] Towner's comparative study between hymnals of various denominations could be expanded to not only examine psalm versifications, but also lament hymns.[67] Finally, a study of the influence of theological and doctrinal emphases such as John Wesley's perfectionism, or "entire sanctification," on the

66. Duke, "Giving Voice to Suffering in Worship," 263–72.

67. Sibley Towner, "'Without Our Aid He Did Us Make,'" in Strawn and Bowen, *God So Near*, 17–34.

hymnody of the period could begin to uncover reasons for the eventual loss of lament in congregational song across the larger spectrum of evangelical life since ca. 1980.

The Psalms and Global Awareness

Attention has been given to persecuted Christians across the world. In order to bring his congregation into greater solidarity with suffering brothers and sisters, American pastor David Platt developed Secret Church gatherings which mimic the private gatherings of believers across the world who must meet in secret in order to practice their faith.[68] Platt has produced teaching videos for use in these gatherings, with the purpose to draw the attention of the American church to the needs of persecuted believers worldwide. While the Secret Church initiative does not address song, it bears a powerful connection to the lament psalms, as the ancient words of the psalmists can give modern believers words to pray that express the sorrows of persecution and the subsequent cry for deliverance. Research into psalm-based global worship songs could serve to augment the work of Platt and of others involved in similar ministry projects.

CONCLUSION

The case studies presented at the opening of this chapter represent the versatility of the psalms of lament for use by individuals and groups, for personal devotional use, and in pastoral care. The parallel studies surveyed demonstrate the interconnectedness of lament with other biblical and theological studies. The complexity of the society and culture in which believers live requires that the cry of suffering not be answered with triumphalist platitudes of prosperity and success, but with the heartfelt expressions found in the ancient words of the psalmists that gave witness to the rich dialogical nature of Israel's relationship with God throughout history.

68. Platt, "Secret Church."

The outpouring of recent artistic work in case studies and parallel studies surrounding the psalmic laments is calling believers to consider their use anew in corporate worship. However, a word of caution is in order. Care must be taken to not allow lament practices to be viewed as a trendy practice that will soon pass out of use, eclipsed by yet a newer trend. Superficial co-opting of lament in corporate worship practice must be avoided. Scholars from across multiple fields must explore this topic through multiple lenses in thoughtful research built on biblical foundations. While certain trends in corporate worship practices may come and go, individual and corporate lament must never go the way of a passing trend. The role of lament was central to the worship life of ancient Israel, for so much of the nation's history proves that it was not a trend, but rather a deeply-rooted biblical practice that must continue to be cultivated faithfully and reverently in the corporate worship of the gathered church of Jesus Christ until He returns.

The need for ongoing study of the use of lament psalms and their application to various contexts resonates in the cries of believers across the world and will not cease until the coming of Christ's kingdom. Events such as the August 2017 race riots in South Carolina by white supremacists and Neo-Nazis directed against African-Americans, massive food insecurity that is gripping so much of the world, and gun violence that takes the lives of school children calls the church to lament, to "weep with those who weep" (Rom 12:15). Isaac Wardell, founder of the Porter's Gate Worship Project, served as director of worship arts at Trinity Presbyterian Church in Charlottesville, VA at the time of the race riots. On the Sunday following the riots, the congregation was invited to gather in small groups to worship and pray together, fostering a spirit of humility and vulnerability. Wardell contends, "simply instructing our people in the need for humility could never be a replacement for the very embodied act of moving toward one another in gentleness."[69] The tension between suffering and hope modeled within the psalms of lament expresses deeply-rooted trust in God who is attentive to the cries of suffering believers. Wherever the

69. Wardell, Isaac. "Reflections from a Charlottesville Church."

common element of fallen humanity is present, believers will need to give voice to suffering. As God's own word, the psalms of lament will never be exhausted, but will continue to serve as the voice of prayer and ultimately of trust and hope for the church of Christ until he returns.

Bibliography

Alberti, Fay Bound. *A Biography of Loneliness: The History of an Emotion*. New York: Oxford University Press, 2019.

Angel, Chris. "Sing a New Song: Songs and Hymns from the Bible." *The Hymn* 68.2 (Spring 2017) 33–34.

Armstrong, Slater. *Even in Sorrow: A Recorded Project for the Persecuted Church in Sudan*. Joining Our Voices. B001CQOQOA. 2002. CD.

Aulén, Gustav. *Christus Victor: An Historical Study of the Three Main Types of the Idea of Atonement*. London: SPCK, 1931.

Austin, J. L. *How to Do Things with Words*. Cambridge: Boston University Press, 1962.

Bader-Saye, Scott. "Fear in the Garden: The State of Emergency and the Politics of Blessing." *Ex Auditu* 24 (2008) 1–13.

Balentine, Samuel E. *Prayer in the Hebrew Bible: The Drama of Divine-Human Dialogue*. Overtures to Biblical Theology. Edited by Walter Brueggemann. Minneapolis: Fortress, 1993.

Beker, J. Christiaan. *Suffering and Hope: The Biblical Vision and the Human Predicament*. Grand Rapids: Eerdmans, 1994.

Best, Ernest. *Second Corinthians*. Interpretation: A Bible Commentary for Teaching & Preaching. Louisville: Westminster John Knox, 1987.

Billman, Kathleen D., and Daniel L. Migliore. *Rachel's Cry: Prayer of Lament and Rebirth of Hope*. Eugene, OR: Wipf & Stock, 2007.

Botha, Eugene J. "Speech Act Theory and Biblical Interpretation." *Neotestamentica* 41.2 (2007) 274–94.

Boyd, Gregory A. *God at War: The Bible and Spiritual Conflict*. Downers Grove: InterVarsity, 1997.

137

Bibliography

Boyle, Gregory. *Tattoos on the Heart: The Power of Boundless Compassion*. New York: Free Press, 2010.

Brackett, Mark. *Permission to Feel: Unlocking the Power of Emotions to Help Our Kids, Ourselves, and Our Society Thrive*. New York: Celedon, 2019.

Brown, Sally A., and Patrick D. Miller, eds. *Lament: Reclaiming Practices in Pulpit, Pew, and Public Square*. Louisville: Westminster John Knox, 2005.

Brueggemann, Walter. "The Costly Loss of Lament." *Journal for the Study of the Old Testament* 36 (October 1986) 57–71.

———. "The Friday Voice of Faith." *Reformed Worship* 30 (December 1993). https://www.reformedworship.org/article/december-1993/ friday-voice-faith-serious-theology-cross-requires-serious-practice-lament-psa.

———. *Hope within History*. Louisville: Westminster John Knox, 1988.

———. *Israel's Praise: Doxology against Idolatry and Ideology*. Philadelphia: Fortress, 1988.

———. *The Message of the Psalms: A Theological Commentary*. Minneapolis: Augsburg, 1984.

———. *Praying the Psalms*. Winona, MN: St. Mary's, 1984.

———. *The Psalms and the Life of Faith*. Edited by Patrick D. Miller. Minneapolis: Fortress, 1995.

———. *Reverberations of Faith: A Theological Handbook of Old Testament Themes*. Louisville: Westminster John Knox, 2002.

———. *Spirituality of the Psalms*. Minneapolis: Fortress, 2002.

Brueggemann, Walter, and William H. Bellinger, Jr. *Psalms*. New Cambridge Bible Commentary. New York: Cambridge University Press, 2014.

Cacioppo, John T. *Loneliness: Human Nature and the Need for Social Connection*. New York: W. W. Norton, 2009.

Card, Michael. "Come Lift Up Your Sorrows." *The Hidden Face of God*, Discovery House Music B000GS5DTY. 2006. CD.

———. "General Session 6, Part 1." Presentation, Think Worship Conference at The Southern Baptist Theological Seminary, Louisville, June 17–19, 2014.

———. *A Sacred Sorrow: Reaching Out to God in the Lost Language of Lament*. Colorado Springs: Nav, 2005.

Carter, Warren. "Matthew 23:27–39." *Interpretation* 54.1 (January 2000) 66–68

"Conversation with Singer-Songwriter Sandra McCracken." Calvin Worship Institute. May 2, 2017. http://worship.calvin.edu/resources/resource-library/conversation-with-singer-songwriter-sandra-mccracken/.

Duff, Nancy. "Recovering Lamentation as a Practice in the Church." In *Lament: Reclaiming Practices in Pulpit, Pew, and Public Square*, edited by Sally A. Brown and Paul D. Miller, 3–14. Louisville: Westminster John Knox, 2005.

Duke, David Nelson. "Giving Voice to Suffering in Worship: A Study in the Theodicies of Hymnody." *Encounter* 52.3 (1991) 263–72.

Eaton, John. *The Psalms: A Historical and Spiritual Commentary with an Introduction and New Translation*. London: T & T Clark, 2003.

Ebel, Jonathan. *Faith in the Fight: Religion and the American Soldier in the Great War*. Princeton, NJ: Princeton University Press, 2010.

Eklund, Rebekah. *Jesus Wept: The Significance of Jesus' Laments in the New Testament*. The Library of New Testament Studies, edited by Mark Goodacre. London: T & T Clark, 2015.

———. *Practicing Lament*. Eugene, OR: Cascade, 2021.

Ellington, Scott. *Risking Truth: Reshaping the World through Prayers of Lament*. Edited by K. C. Hanson, Charles M. Collier, and D. Christopher Spinks. Eugene, OR: Pickwick, 2008.

Erickson, Millard. *Christian Theology*. Grand Rapids: Baker, 1985.

Estes, Daniel. "Psalm 78:1–8 as a Musical Intertext of Torah and Wisdom." *Bibliotheca Sacra* 173 (July–September 2016) 297–314.

Evans, Donald. *The Logic of Self-Involvement: A Philosophical Study of Everyday Language with Special Reference to the Christian Use of Language about God as Creator*. Edited by Ronald Gregor Smith. Norwich, UK: SCM, 1963.

Fiddes, Paul S. *Past Event and Present Salvation: The Christian Idea of Atonement*. Louisville: Westminster John Knox, 1989.

Foster, Robert L., and David M. Howard, eds. *"My Words Are Lovely": Studies in the Rhetoric of the Psalms*. The Library of Hebrew Bible, Old Testament Studies 467. New York: T & T Clark, 2008.

Goldingay, John. *Old Testament Theology: Israel's Life*. Old Testament Theology Series 3. Downers Grove: InterVarsity Academic, 2016.

Goroncy, Jason. *Tikkun Olam: To Mend the World; A Confluence of Theology and the Arts*. Eugene, OR: Pickwick, 2014.

Greenberg, Moshe. *Biblical Prose Prayer*. Berkeley: University of California, 1983.

Grice, Herbert Paul. *Studies in the Way of Words*. Cambridge, MA: Harvard University Press, 2001.

Grudem, Wayne. *1 Peter*. Tyndale New Testament Commentary. Grand Rapids: Eerdmans, 1988.

Gunkel, Hermann. *The Psalms: A Form-Critical Introduction*. Philadelphia: Fortress, 1967.

Hall, Douglas. *God and Human Suffering: An Exercise in the Theology of the Cross*. Minneapolis: Augsburg, 1986.

Harper, Brad. "Christus Victor, Postmodernism, and the Shaping of Atonement Theology." *Cultural Encounters* 2.1 (2005) 37–51.

Harrison Warren, Tish. *A Prayer in the Night: For Those Who Work or Watch or Weep*. Downers Grove, InterVarsity, 2021.

Hays, Richard B. *Echoes of Scripture in the Letters of Paul*. New Haven, CT: Yale University Press, 1989.

Hiebert, D. Edmond. *First Peter: An Expositional Commentary*. Chicago: Moody, 1984.

"Illocutionary Act." *Oxford Living Dictionary*. https://www.oxfordreference.com/view/10.1093/oi/authority.20110803095957841.

Johnson, Eric. *Foundations for Soul Care: A Christian Psychology Approach*. Downers Grove: InterVarsity, 2007.

Keener, Craig. *Romans*. New Covenant Commentary Series. Eugene, OR: Cascade, 2009.

Bibliography

Keesmaat, Sylvia C. "Paul and His Story: (Re)Interpreting the Exodus Tradition." *Journal for the Study of the New Testament.*

Keller, Timothy. *Hope in Times of Fear: The Resurrection and the Meaning of Easter.* New York: Viking, 2021.

———. "Praying the Gospel." *Psalms: The Songs of Jesus* sermon series. Recorded February 20–March 19, 2000. Redeemer Presbyterian Church, New York. http://www.gospelinlife.com/psalms-the-songs-of-jesus.

———. "Praying Your Guilt." *Psalms: The Songs of Jesus* sermon series. Recorded February 20–March 19, 2000. Redeemer Presbyterian Church, New York. http://www.gospelinlife.com/psalms-the-songs-of-jesus.

———. "Praying Your Tears." *Psalms: The Songs of Jesus* sermon series. Recorded February 20–March 19, 2000. Redeemer Presbyterian Church, New York. http://www.gospelinlife.com/psalms-the-songs-of-jesus.

———. "Suffering: If God Is Good, Why Is There So Much Evil in the World?" Sermon series. Recorded October 1, 2006. Redeemer Presbyterian Church, New York. http://www.gospelinlife.com/suffering-if-god-is-good-why-is-there-so-much-evil-in-the-world-5495.

———. *Walking with God through Pain and Suffering.* New York: Dutton, 2013.

Kitamori, Kazoh. *Theology of the Pain of God.* Richmond, VA: John Knox, 1965.

Koyama, Kosuke. *Mount Fuji and Mount Sinai: A Critique of Idols.* Maryknoll, NY: Orbis, 1985.

Krabill, James R, ed. *Worship and Mission for the Global Church: An Ethnodoxology Handbook.* Pasadena: William Carey Library, 2013.

Lane, Timothy S., and Paul David Tripp. *How People Change.* Greensboro, NC: New Growth, 2006.

Lepore, Jill. "The History of Loneliness." *The New Yorker,* April 6, 2020. https://www.newyorker.com/magazine/2020/04/06/the-history-of-loneliness.

Long, Thomas G. "Four Ways to Preach a Psalm." *Journal for Preachers* 37.2 (Lent 2014) 21–32.

Longman, Tremper, III. *Psalms.* Tyndale Old Testament Commentaries. Downers Grove: InterVarsity, 2014.

Marohnic, Chuck. "Psalms Reborn." Music Serving the World Ministries. https://www.wordreborn.com/psalms-reborn.

Martin, Lee Roy. *Toward a Pentecostal Theology of Worship.* Edited by Lee Roy Martin. Cleveland, TN: CPT, 2016.

Mays, James Luther. *The Lord Reigns: A Theological Handbook to the Psalms.* Louisville: Westminster John Knox, 1994.

———. "Prayer and Christology: Psalm 22 as Perspective on the Passion." *Theology Today* 42.3 (October 1985) 322–31.

———. *Psalms.* Interpretation. Louisville: Westminster John Knox, 1994.

McCann, J. Clinton. *A Theological Introduction to the Book of Psalms: The Psalms as Torah.* Nashville: Abingdon, 1993.

McCartney, Dan G. "Suffering and the Goodness of God in the Gospels." In *Suffering and the Goodness of God,* edited by Christopher W. Morgan and Robert A. Peterson, 79–94. Theology in Community. Wheaton, IL: Crossway, 2008.

Bibliography

McCracken, Sandra. *Psalms*. Towhee Records B00U583Z9U, 2015. CD.

———. "Songs of Praise, Lament, and Hope." Lecture, Calvin Institute of Worship, May 2, 2016. http://worship.calvin.edu/resources/resource-library/songs-of-praise-lament-and-hope/.

Mesa, Ivan. "Sandra McCracken on Life, Loss, and Longing in the Psalms." May 21, 2015. https://www.thegospelcoalition.org/article/sandra-mccracken-psalms.

Miller, Patrick D. *They Cried to the Lord: The Form and Theology of Biblical Prayer*. Minneapolis: Fortress, 1994.

Morgan, Christopher W., and Robert A. Peterson, eds. *Suffering and the Goodness of God*. Theology in Community. Wheaton, IL: Crossway, 2008.

Mouw, Richard J. "Why Christus Victor Is Not Enough: Each Atonement Theory Highlights a Truth about the Cross—But None More So Than Christ's Substitutionary Death." *Christianity Today* 56.5 (May 2012) 28–31.

Mouw, Richard J., and Douglas Sweeney. *The Suffering and Victorious Christ: Toward a More Compassionate Christology*. Grand Rapids: Baker, 2013.

Moyise, Steve, and Maarten J. J. Menken. "Introduction," 1-3. In *The Psalms in the New Testament*, edited by Steve Moyise and Maarten J. J. Menken. New York: T & T Clark, 2004.

Murthy, Vivek. *Together: The Healing Power of Human Connection in a Sometimes Lonely World*. New York: Harper Wave, 2020.

Nichols, Stephen J. *Jesus Made in America: A Cultural History from the Puritans to "The Passion of the Christ."* Downers Grove: InterVarsity, 2008.

Nowell, Irene. *Pleading, Cursing, Praising: Conversing with God through the Psalms*. Collegeville, MN: Liturgical, 2013.

O'Day, Gail. "Surprised by Faith: Jesus and the Canaanite Woman." *Listening* 24.3 (Fall 1989) 290–301.

Otten, Liam. "'Requiem of Light' in Forest Park April 23." https://source.wustl.edu/2022/04/requiem-of-light-in-forest-park-april-23/.

Otten, Liam, and Byard, James. "Requiem of Light." https://source.wustl.edu/2022/06/requiem-of-light/.

Pemberton, Ben. *Hurting with God: Learning to Lament with the Psalms*. Abilene, TX: Abilene Christian University Press, 2012.

Peterman, Gerald W., and Andrew J. Schmutzer. *Between Pain and Grace: A Biblical Theology of Suffering*. Chicago: Moody, 2016.

Pierce, Timothy M. *Enthroned on our Praise: An Old Testament Theology of Worship*. NAC Studies in Bible and Theology. Nashville: B & H, 2008.

Platt, David. "Secret Church." http://www.radical.net/about-secret-church.

Plummer, Robert L. "The Role of Suffering in the Mission of Paul and the Mission of the Church." *The Southern Baptist Journey of Theology* 17, no. 4 (Winter 2013) 6–19.

Powery, Luke. "Painful Praise: Exploring the Public Proclamation of the Hymns of Revelation." *Theology Today* 70.1 (2013) 69–78.

The Psalms Project. "Psalms 1–10." Vol. 1. December 20, 2011. https://hypeddit.com/link/it7ofh.

———. "Psalms 11–20." Vol. 2. December 10, 2013. https://hypeddit.com/link/imnomc.

———. "Psalms 21–30." Vol. 3. N.d. https://hypeddit.com/link/4itwrk.

Saliers, Don. *The Soul in Paraphrase: Prayer and the Religious Affections.* New York: Seabury, 1980.

———. *Worship as Theology: Foretaste of Glory Divine.* Nashville: Abingdon, 1994.

Schmutzer, Andrew J., and David M. Howard, Jr. *The Psalms: Language for All Seasons of the Soul.* Chicago: Moody, 2013.

Schreiner, Thomas R. *Paul: Apostle of God's Glory in Christ.* Downers Grove: InterVarsity, 2001.

Searle, John. *Expression and Meaning: Studies in the Theory of Speech Acts.* Cambridge, MA: Harvard University Press, 1979.

———. *Speech Acts: An Essay in the Philosophy of Language.* Cambridge: Harvard University Press, 1969.

Shillito, Edward. "Jesus of the Scars." In *Jesus of the Scars: And Other Poems.* London: Hodder and Stoughton, 1919.

Smith, Martyn John. *Divine Violence and the Christus Victor Atonement Model: God's Reluctant Use of Violence for Soteriological Ends.* Eugene, OR: Pickwick, 2016.

Smith, C., Christopher and John Pattison. *Slow Church: Cultivating Community in the Patient Way of Jesus.* Downers Grove: InterVarsity, 2014.

Strawn, Brent A. and Nancy R. Bowen, eds. *A God So Near: Essays on Old Testament Theology in Honor of Patrick D. Miller.* Winona Lake, IN: Eisenbrauns, 2003

Swinton, John. *Finding Jesus in the Storm: The Spiritual Lives of Christians with Mental Health Challenges.* Grand Rapids: Eerdmans, 2020.

———. *Raging with Compassion: Pastoral Care Responses to the Problem of Evil.* Grand Rapids: Eerdmans, 2007.

Thompson, Curt. *Anatomy of the Soul: Surprising Connections between Neuroscience and Spiritual Practices That Can Transform Your Life and Relationships.* Carol Stream, IL: Tyndale, 2010.

Villanueva, Federico G. *The "Uncertainty of a Hearing": A Study of the Sudden Change of Mood in the Psalms of Lament.* Leiden, The Netherlands: Brill, 2008.

Waltke, Bruce K., et al. *The Psalms as Christian Lament: A Historical Commentary.* Grand Rapids: Eerdmans, 2014.

Wardell, Isaac. "Reflections from a Charlottesville Church." Calvin Institute of Christian Worship, August 28, 2017. https://worship.calvin.edu/resources/resource-library/reflections-from-a-charlottesville-church/.

Webber, Robert E. *Ancient-Future Faith: Rethinking Evangelicalism for a Post-Modern World.* Grand Rapids: Baker, 1999.

Wells, C. Richard, and Ray Van Neste. *Forgotten Songs: Reclaiming the Psalms for Christian Worship.* Nashville: B & H, 2012.

Bibliography

"WHO Coronavirus (COVID-19) Dashboard." World Health Organization, Revised July 8, 2022. https://covid19.who.int/.

Wenham, Gordon. *Psalms as Torah: Reading Biblical Song Ethically.* Grand Rapids: Baker, 2012.

Westerholm, Matthew. "'The Hour Is Coming and Is Now Here': The Doctrine of Inaugurated Eschatology in Contemporary Evangelical Worship Music." PhD diss., The Southern Baptist Theological Seminary, 2016.

Westermann, Claus. *Praise and Lament in the Psalms.* Atlanta: John Knox, 1985.

———. "The Role of Lament in the Theology of the Old Testament." *Interpretation* 28.1 (1974) 20–38.

Witvliet, John. *The Biblical Psalms in Christian Worship: A Brief Introduction and Guide to Resources.* Grand Rapids: Eerdmans, 2007.

———. *Worship Seeking Understanding: Windows into Christian Practice.* Grand Rapids: Baker, 2003.

Wolterstorff, Nicholas. *Lament for a Son.* Grand Rapids: Eerdmans, 1987.

"World Watch List." Open Doors USA. https://www.opendoorsusa.org/christian-persecution/world-watch-list/.

Wright, N. T. *The Case for the Psalms: Why They Are Essential.* New York: Harper One, 2013.

Zaretsky, Robert. *The Subversive Simone Weil.* Chicago: University of Chicago Press, 2021.